OPERATION: MORNINGSTAR

Report of Proceedings

QUEEN & COUNTRY

OPERATION: MORNINGSTAR

Report of Proceedings

compiled by **GREG RUCKA**

pencilled by **BRIAN HURTT**

chapter 1 inked by
BRYAN O'MALLEY

chapters 2-3 inked by
CHRISTINE NORRIE

chapter breaks by
JOHN K. SNYDER III

cover by
DURWIN TALON

lettering by
SEAN KONOT

introduction by
STUART MOORE

book design by
KEITH WOOD

collection edited by
JAMIE S. RICH

original series edited by
JAMIE S. RICH & JAMES LUCAS JONES

Published by Oni Press, Inc.
JOE NOZEMACK, publisher
JAMES LUCAS JONES, editor in chief
RANDAL C. JARRELL, managing editor
MARYANNE SNELL, director of sales & marketing

Original Queen & Country logo designed by
STEVEN BIRCH @ Servo

This collects issues 5-7 of the Oni Press comics series *Queen & Country*™.

ONI PRESS, INC.
1305 SE Martin Luther King Jr. Blvd
Suite A
Portland, OR 97214

www.onipress.com

First edition: September 2002
ISBN 1-929998-35-X

3 5 7 9 10 8 6 4

PRINTED IN CANADA.

John K. Snyder would like to thank
Carol Hilliard and Ashan Haq for posing,
and Bain Zietlow and the staff at Animators
at Law for helping out with the scans.

INTRODUCTION

by **STUART MOORE**

I remember Greg Rucka leaning forward over the convention table, telling me about Afghanistan. He'd been trying to decide on a plot for the second arc of his new comic book, *Queen & Country*. His wife, the very talented Jen Van Meter, had suggested to him that he always did his best work when he wrote about something that made him angry. And the Taleban regime—its human rights abuses, its endorsement of international terrorism, and particularly its treatment of women—made him very, very angry.

Not an unusual conversation—except that this took place in *July* 2001.

Now, I like to pretend I'm a worldly person. I've studied American politics, and I keep up pretty well with U.S. events and technological developments. But I have to admit that, like most Americans a short year ago, I was pretty woefully out of touch with foreign affairs. I was vaguely aware that some pretty bad things were going on in Afghanistan, but I'd barely heard of the Taleban.

Then Al Qaeda terrorists killed thousands of people in New York—*my* city, barely three miles from my home in Brooklyn. And I found myself stunned and unprepared, frankly ignorant of the forces that had brought about this tragedy.

But Greg had done his research. *Queen & Country: Morningstar*, which was about to begin, would send the series' "Minders" straight into the heart of Afghanistan. Which brought up an interesting question: What part could British secret service agent Tara Chace, *Queen & Country's* central protagonist, play in a mission to a country where the regime routinely encouraged men to beat their spouses to death for violating the smallest rule? It's that question, as much as anything, that sets *Morningstar* in motion.

By the time the story was published, of course, the English-speaking world had changed. The Taleban was a household word, to the point where comics fans complained that it was spelled wrong in the comic (the media having universally adopted the equally-valid spelling "Taliban"). And *Queen & Country* looked like it was either jumping on a media bandwagon, or prescient.

It was the second. Make no mistake: This is a pre-9/11 story. Its concerns are those of an international community trying to deal with a difficult situation without stirring the pot too much. Of course, by the time of the *next arc* of *Queen & Country*, the Taleban had fallen, and the mere idea of "infiltrating" Afghanistan wouldn't have made any sense. The international playing field was completely different—and that, too, was reflected in the comic.

Like many Americans, I'm ashamed that I didn't pay enough attention to the grave international tensions that brought about the tragedy of 9/11. Isolationism just doesn't cut it in today's small world, and it's important for all of us to keep an eye on what our neighbors—and our leaders—are doing. That applies to a Washington administration that uses national crises to bolster big oil interests as much as it does to rival superpowers, or to still-neglected areas of mass strife like Uganda or Rwanda.

Now, *Queen & Country* isn't a political tract. It's an international thriller, full of dirty deeds, hard people, and harder decisions. And Tara Chace is a fascinating character, still haunted by her actions in *Operation: Broken Ground*, where she was sent to deliberately assassinate a Russian general.

But when a comic is set against a backdrop of international intrigue, it's impressive when that comic hits something on the head as solidly as this one did. And I'm grateful to Greg Rucka, and his talented collaborators Brian Hurtt, Bryan O'Malley, and Christine Norrie, for keeping an eye on a crucial part of the world when I wasn't.

Stuart Moore
Brooklyn, New York
August 2002

Stuart Moore has been a writer, a book editor, a kitchen worker, an award-winning comics editor, and the nighttime manager of the Lawrenceville, N.J. Woolworth's curtain department. At DC Comics, he was a founding editor of the acclaimed Vertigo imprint, and from late 2000 through mid-2002 he edited the Marvel Knights comics line and many of the revitalized titles in Marvel's new MAX line. Currently, Stuart freelances as a writer of comic books and essays; he'd like you all to go out and buy Zendra, *the well-reviewed series from Penny-Farthing Press, on sale now. Sadly, there's no going back to Woolworth's—but that hasn't been a problem yet. His fingers are crossed.*

CHAPTER 1

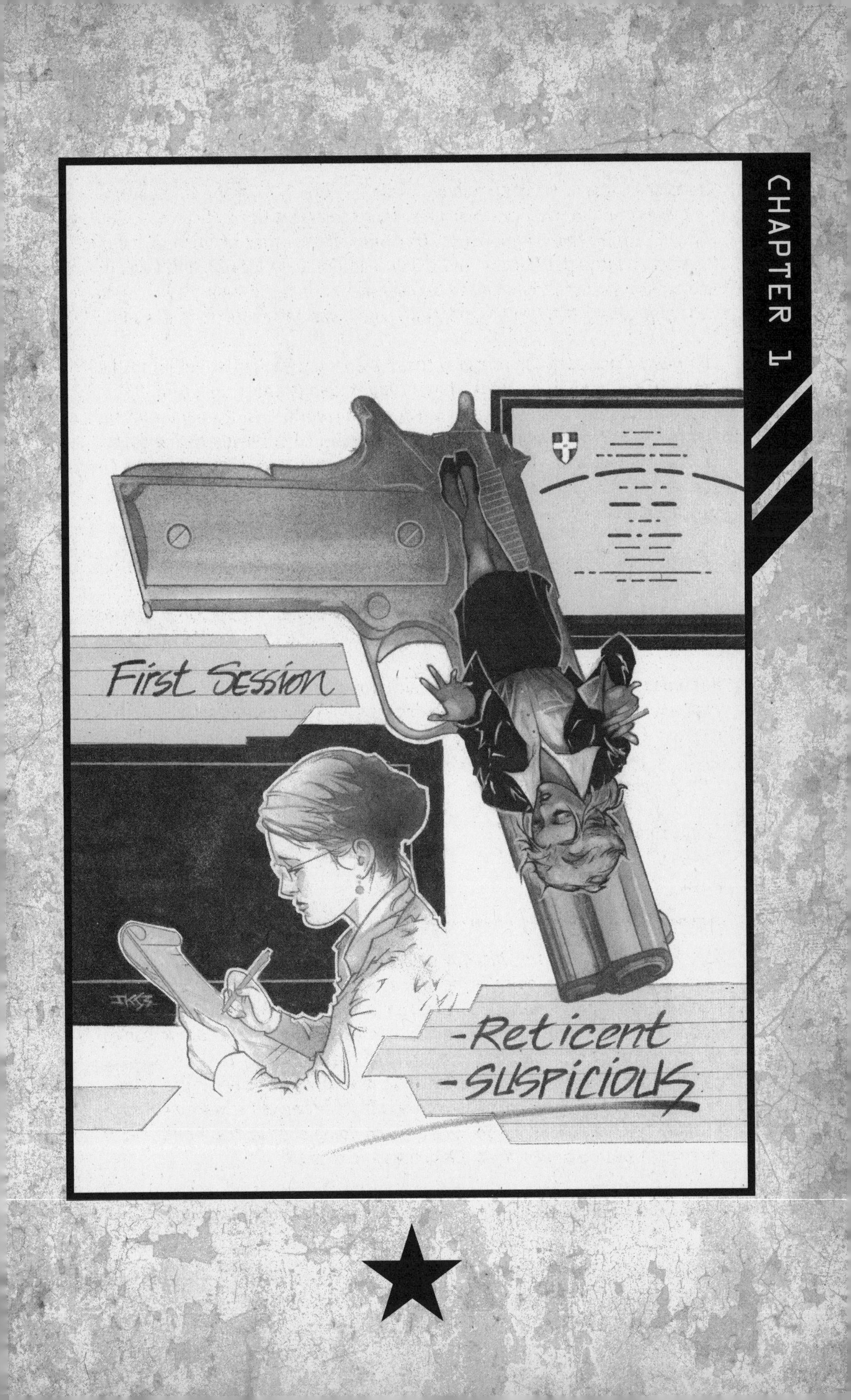
First Session
-Reticent
-SUSPICIOUS

ROSTER

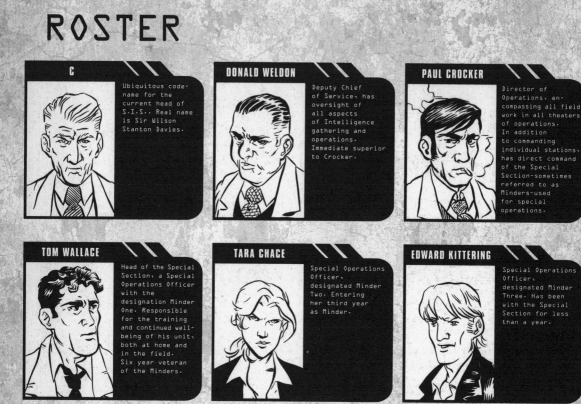

C

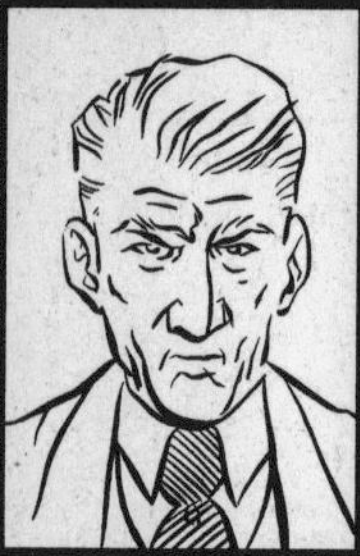

Ubiquitous code-name for the current head of S.I.S.. Real name is Sir Wilson Stanton Davies.

DONALD WELDON

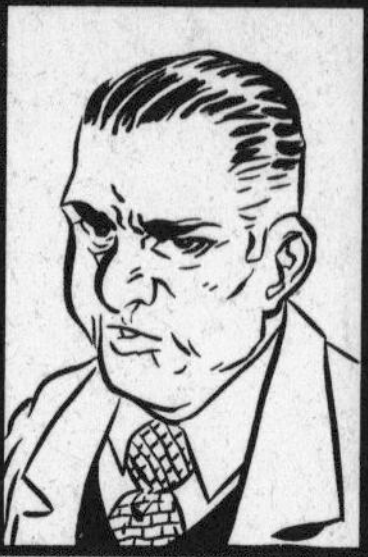

Deputy Chief of Service, has oversight of all aspects of Intelligence gathering and operations. Immediate superior to Crocker.

PAUL CROCKER

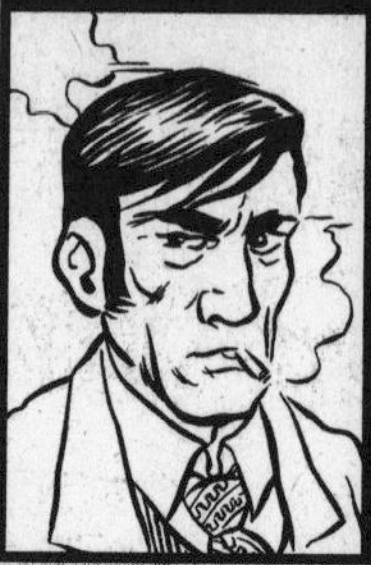

Director of Operations, encompassing all field work in all theaters of operations. In addition to commanding individual stations, has direct command of the Special Section-sometimes referred to as Minders-used for special operations.

TOM WALLACE

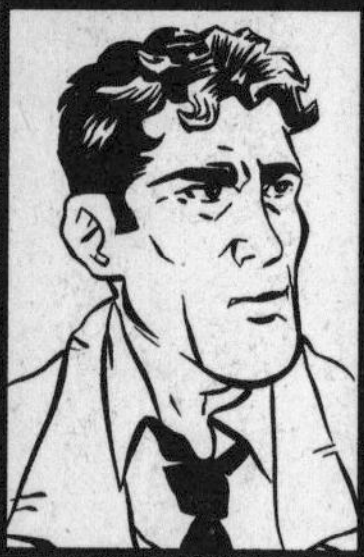

Head of the Special Section, a Special Operations Officer with the designation Minder One. Responsible for the training and continued well-being of his unit, both at home and in the field. Six year veteran of the Minders.

TARA CHACE

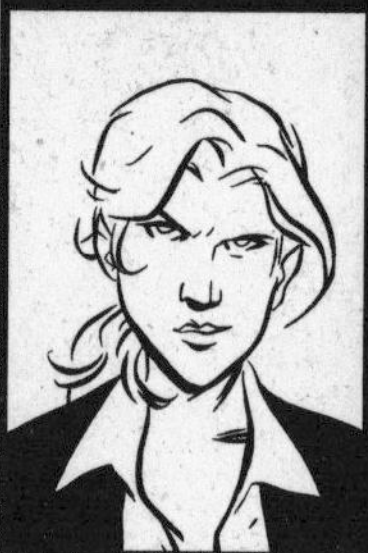

Special Operations Officer, designated Minder Two. Entering her third year as Minder.

EDWARD KITTERING

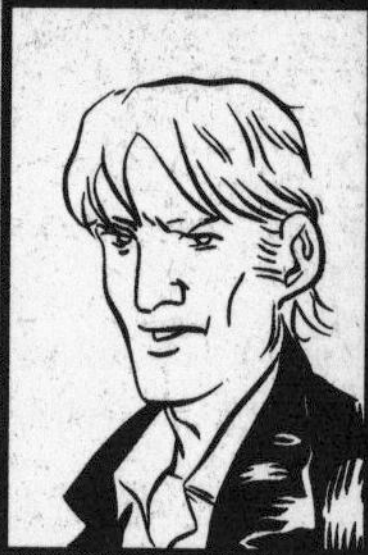

Special Operations Officer, designated Minder Three. Has been with the Special Section for less than a year.

OPS ROOM STAFF:

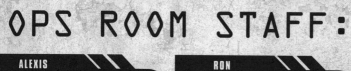

ALEXIS

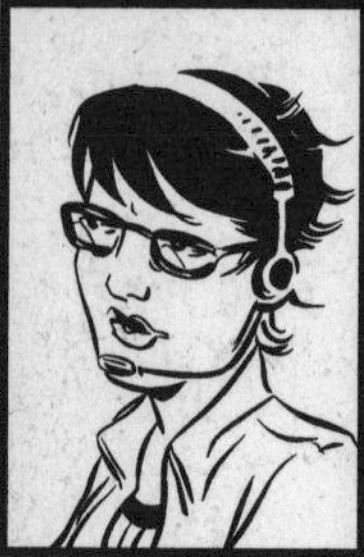

Mission Control Officer (also called Main Communications Officer)-responsible for maintaining communications between the Operations Room and the agents in the field.

RON

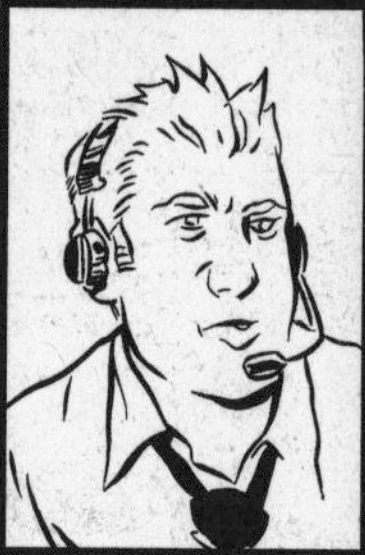

Duty Operations Officer, responsible for monitoring the status and importance of all incoming intelligence, both from foreign stations and other sources.

KATE

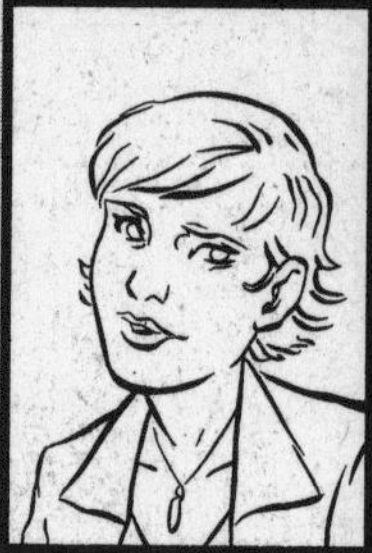

Personal Assistant to Paul Crocker, termed P.A. to D.Ops. Possibly the hardest and most important job in the Service.

OTHERS:

ANGELA CHANG

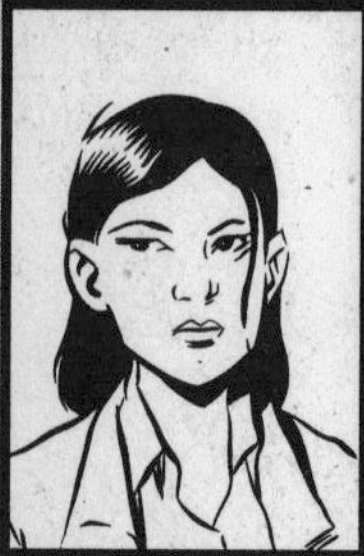

CIA Station Chief in London. Has an unofficial intelligence-sharing arrangement with Crocker.

SIMON RAYBURN

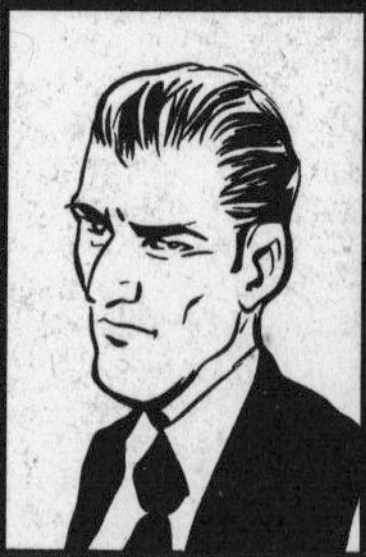

Director of Intelligence for S.I.S. (D. Int), essentially Crocker's opposite number. Responsible for the evaluation, interpretation, and dissemination of all acquired intelligence.

DAVID KINNY

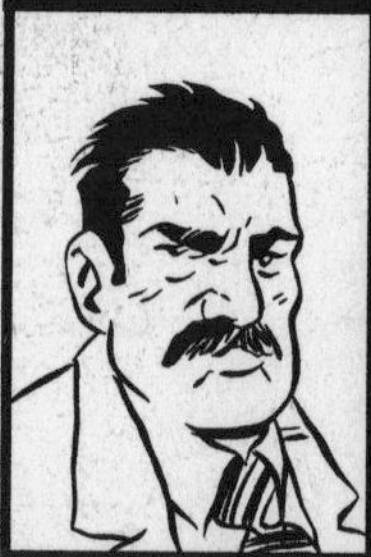

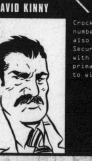

Crocker's opposite number at M.I.5, also called the Security Services, with jurisdiction primarily confined to within the U.K.

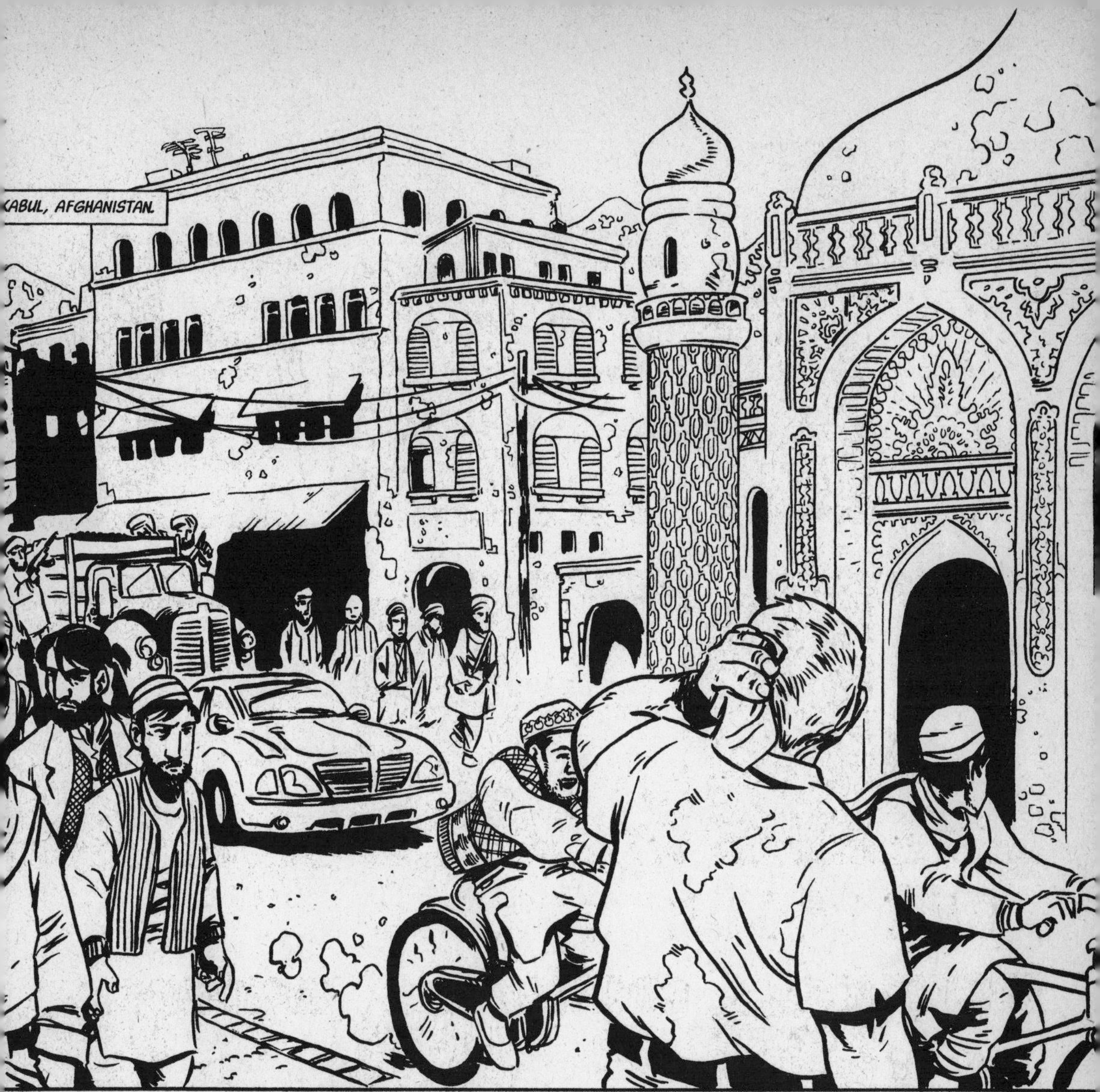
KABUL, AFGHANISTAN.
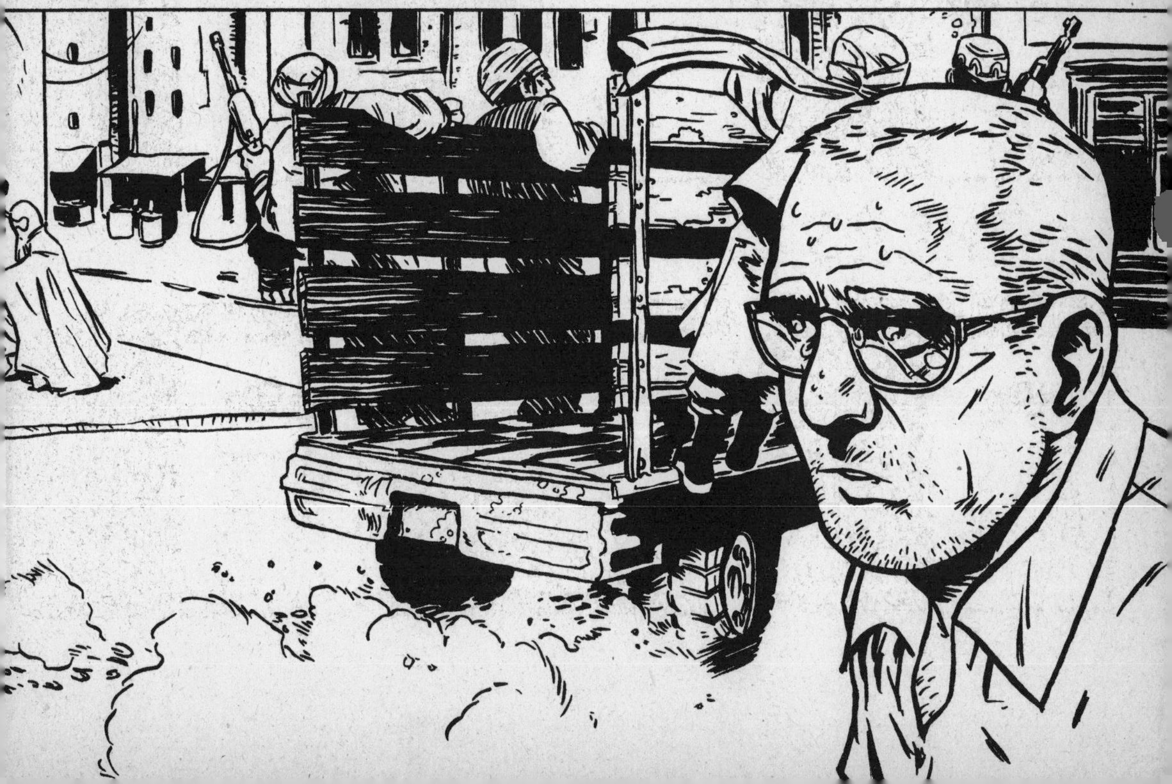

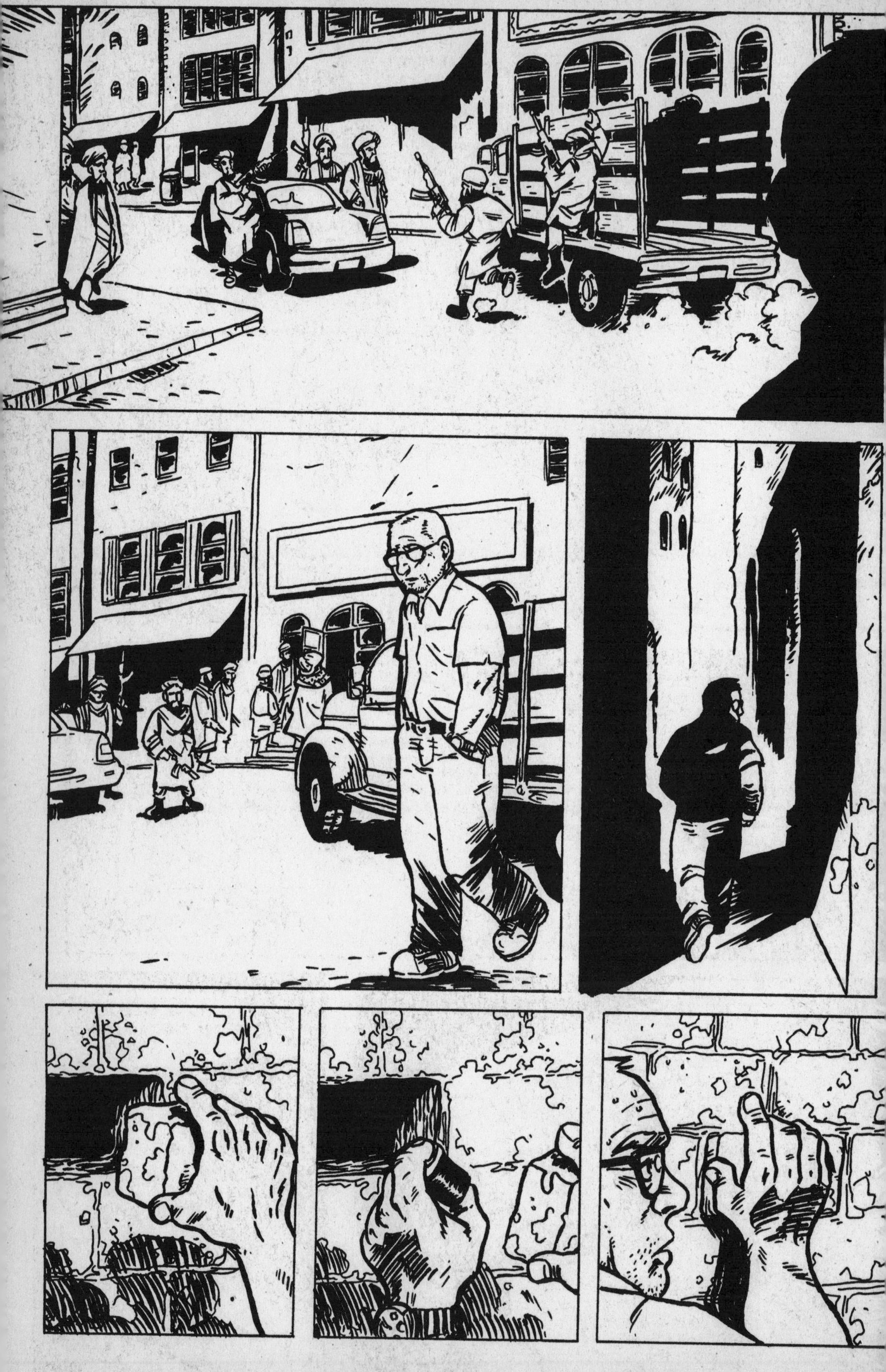

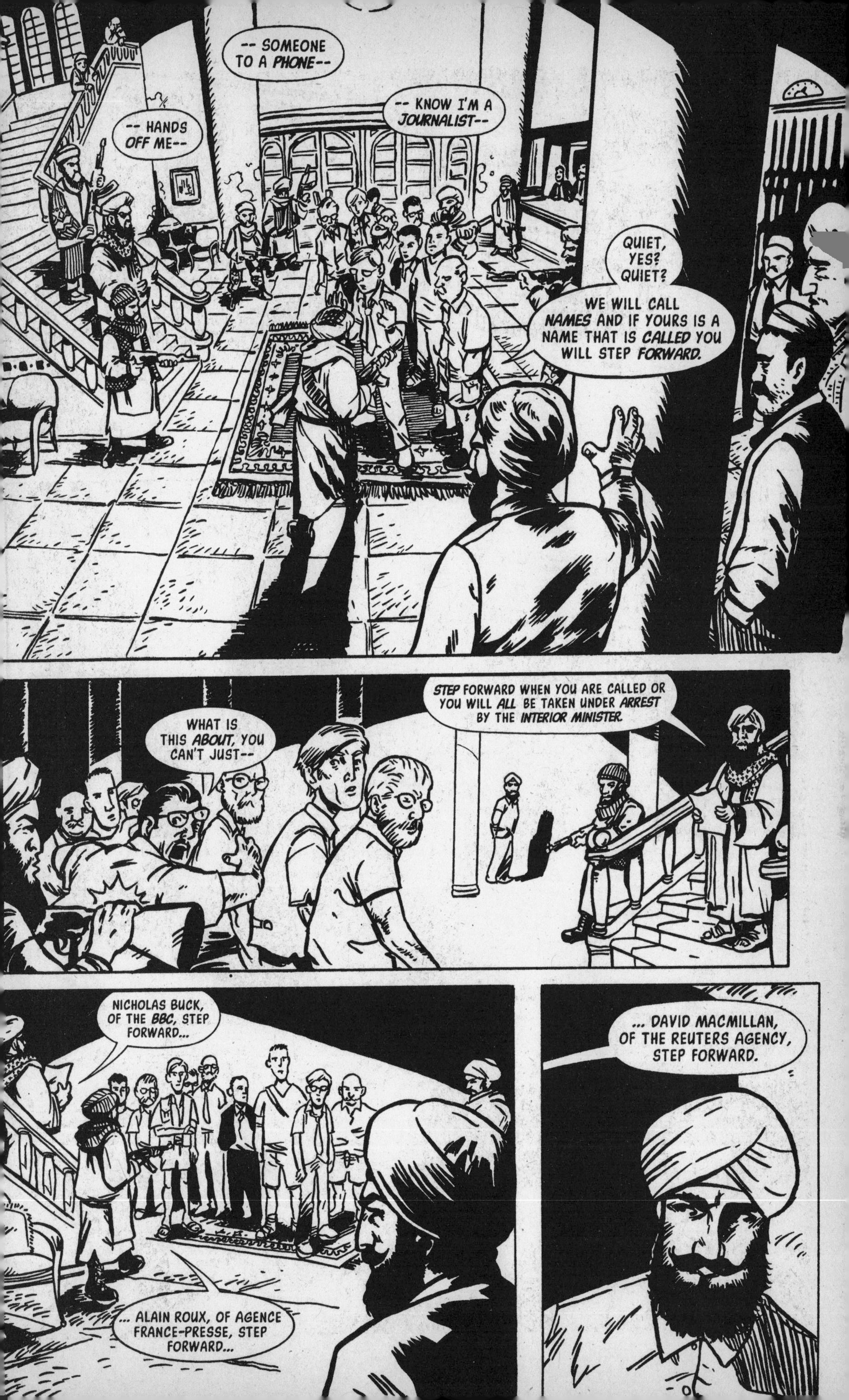
-- HANDS OFF ME--
-- SOMEONE TO A PHONE--
-- KNOW I'M A JOURNALIST--
QUIET, YES? QUIET?
WE WILL CALL NAMES AND IF YOURS IS A NAME THAT IS CALLED YOU WILL STEP FORWARD.
WHAT IS THIS ABOUT, YOU CAN'T JUST--
STEP FORWARD WHEN YOU ARE CALLED OR YOU WILL ALL BE TAKEN UNDER ARREST BY THE INTERIOR MINISTER.
NICHOLAS BUCK, OF THE BBC, STEP FORWARD...
... ALAIN ROUX, OF AGENCE FRANCE-PRESSE, STEP FORWARD...
... DAVID MACMILLAN, OF THE REUTERS AGENCY, STEP FORWARD.

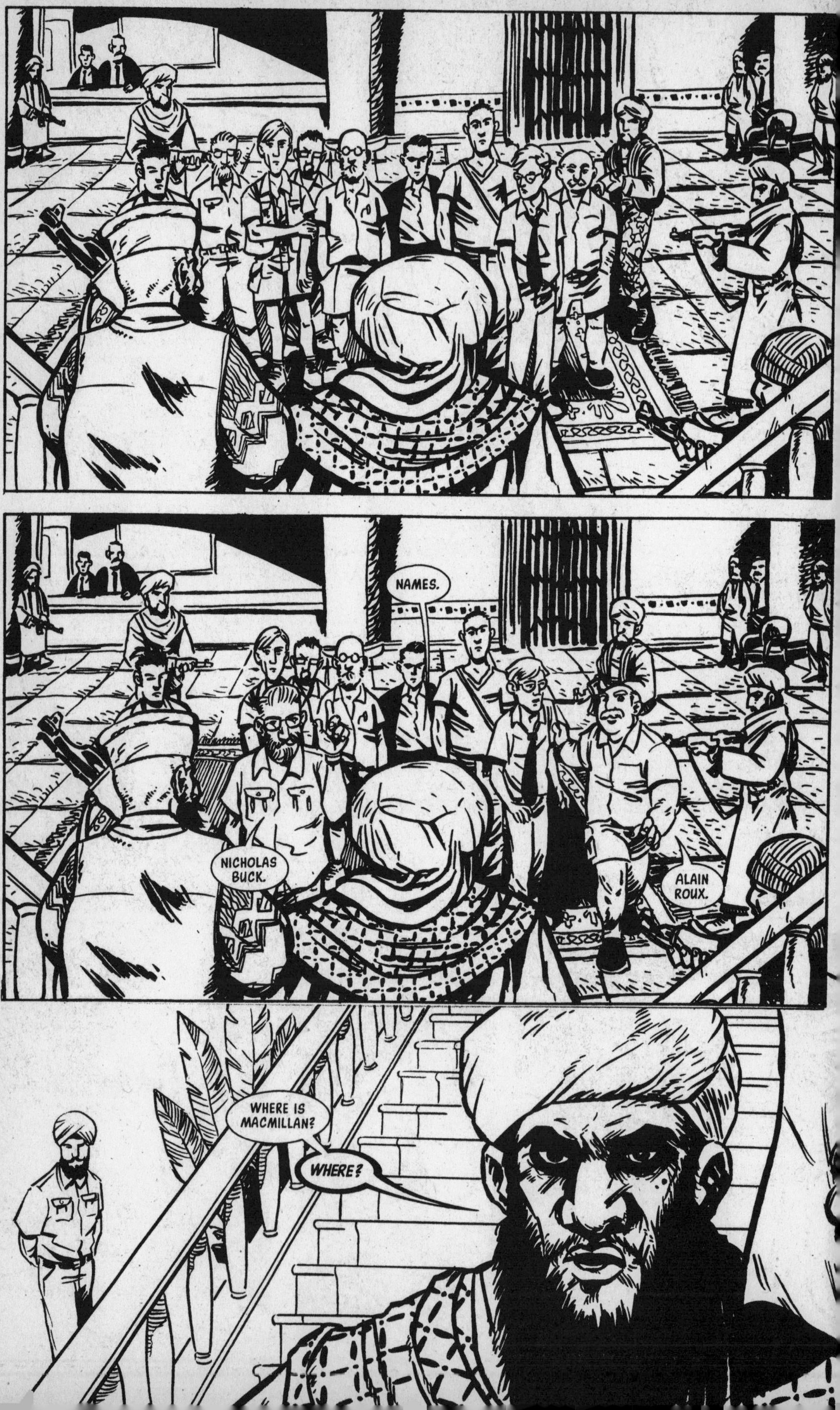
NAMES.
NICHOLAS BUCK.
ALAIN ROUX.
WHERE IS MACMILLAN?
WHERE?

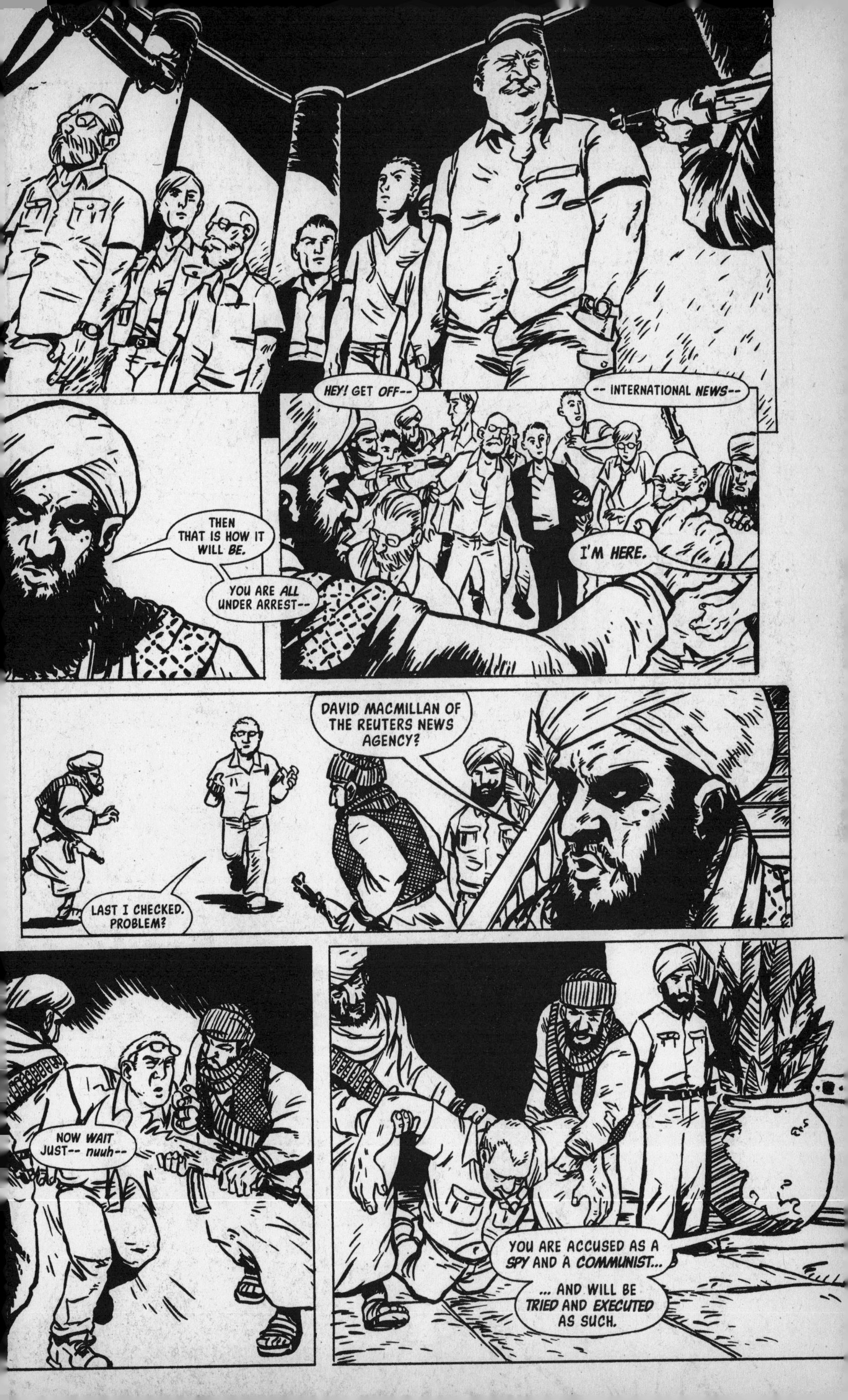
HEY! GET OFF--
-- INTERNATIONAL NEWS--
THEN THAT IS HOW IT WILL BE.
YOU ARE ALL UNDER ARREST--
I'M HERE.
DAVID MACMILLAN OF THE REUTERS NEWS AGENCY?
LAST I CHECKED. PROBLEM?
NOW WAIT JUST-- nuuh--
YOU ARE ACCUSED AS A SPY AND A COMMUNIST...
... AND WILL BE TRIED AND EXECUTED AS SUCH.

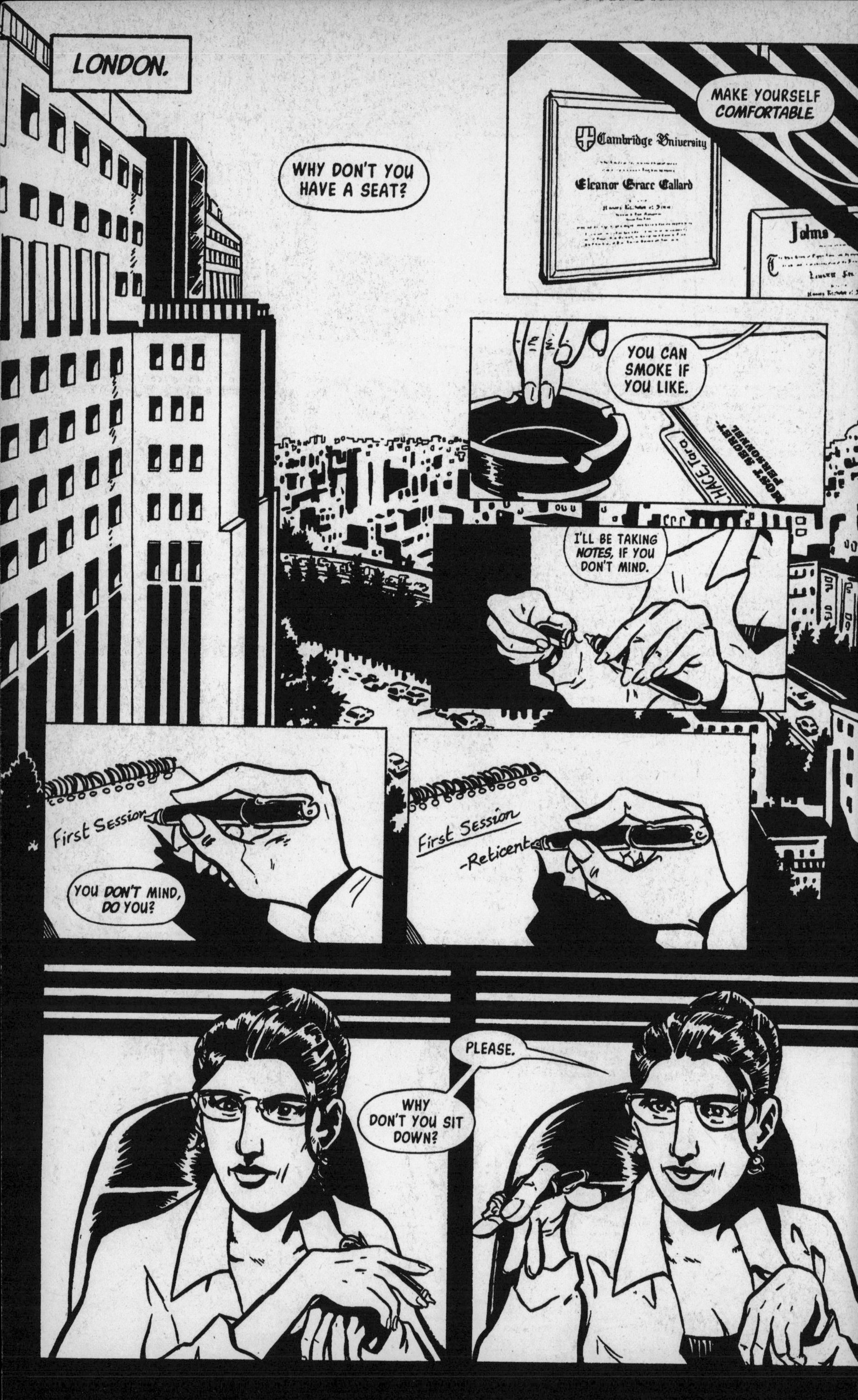
LONDON.
WHY DON'T YOU HAVE A SEAT?
MAKE YOURSELF COMFORTABLE.
Cambridge University
Eleanor Grace Callard
YOU CAN SMOKE IF YOU LIKE.
I'LL BE TAKING NOTES, IF YOU DON'T MIND.
First Session
YOU DON'T MIND, DO YOU?
First Session
-Reticent
WHY DON'T YOU SIT DOWN?
PLEASE.

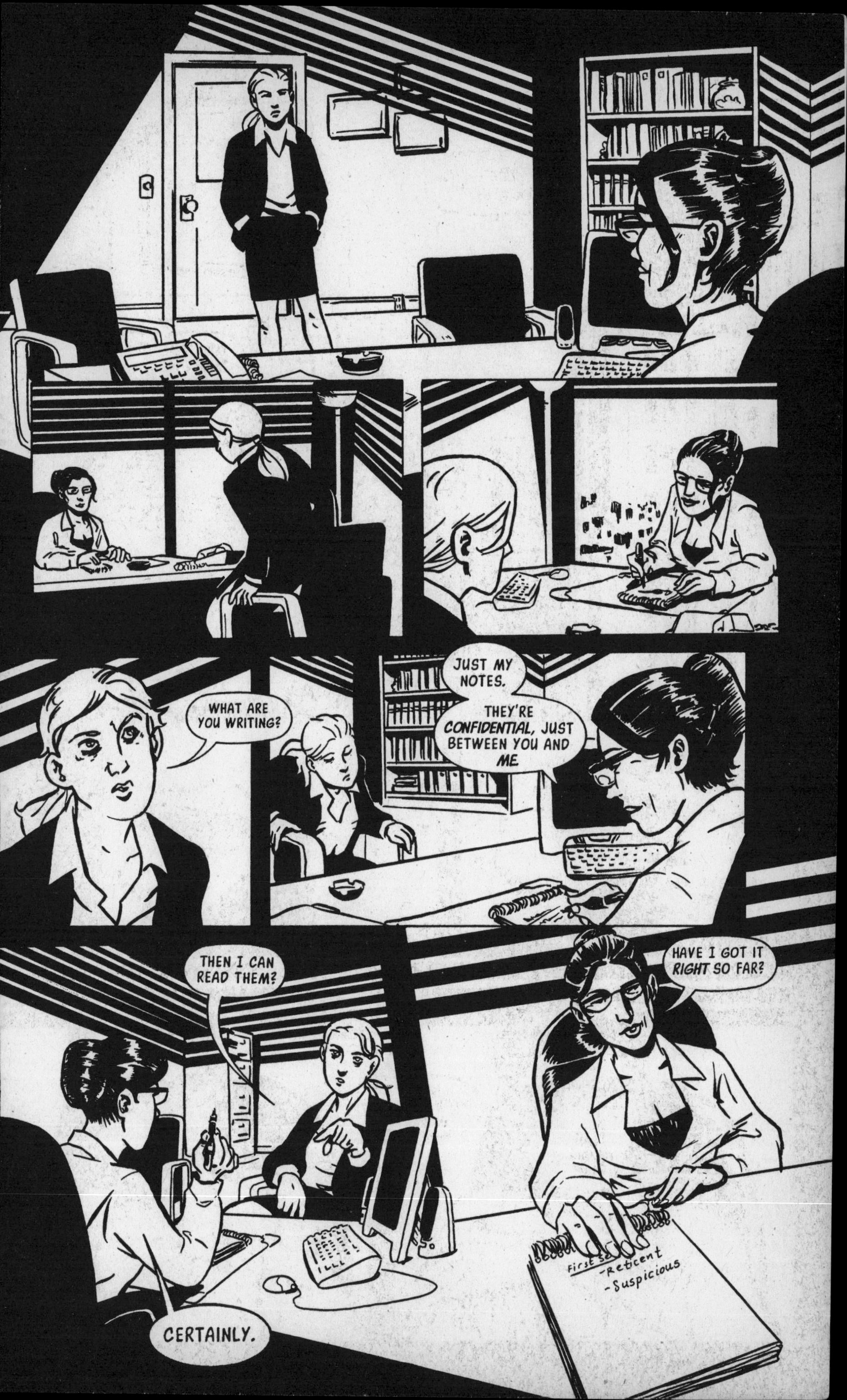
WHAT ARE YOU WRITING?
JUST MY NOTES.
THEY'RE CONFIDENTIAL, JUST BETWEEN YOU AND ME.
THEN I CAN READ THEM?
CERTAINLY.
HAVE I GOT IT RIGHT SO FAR?
-Reticent
-Suspicious

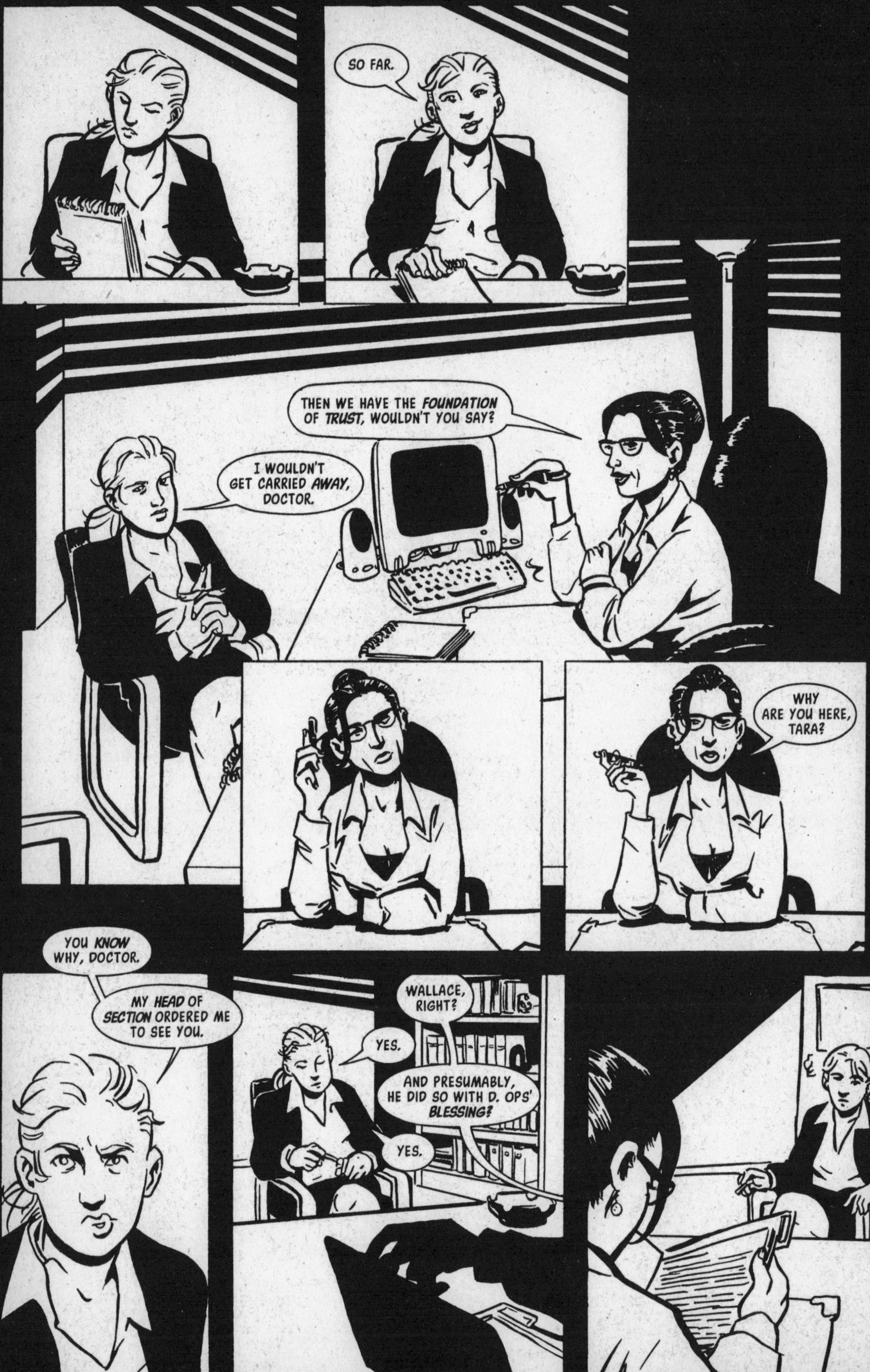
SO FAR.
THEN WE HAVE THE FOUNDATION OF TRUST, WOULDN'T YOU SAY?
I WOULDN'T GET CARRIED AWAY, DOCTOR.
WHY ARE YOU HERE, TARA?
YOU KNOW WHY, DOCTOR.
MY HEAD OF SECTION ORDERED ME TO SEE YOU.
WALLACE, RIGHT?
YES.
AND PRESUMABLY, HE DID SO WITH D. OPS' BLESSING?
YES.

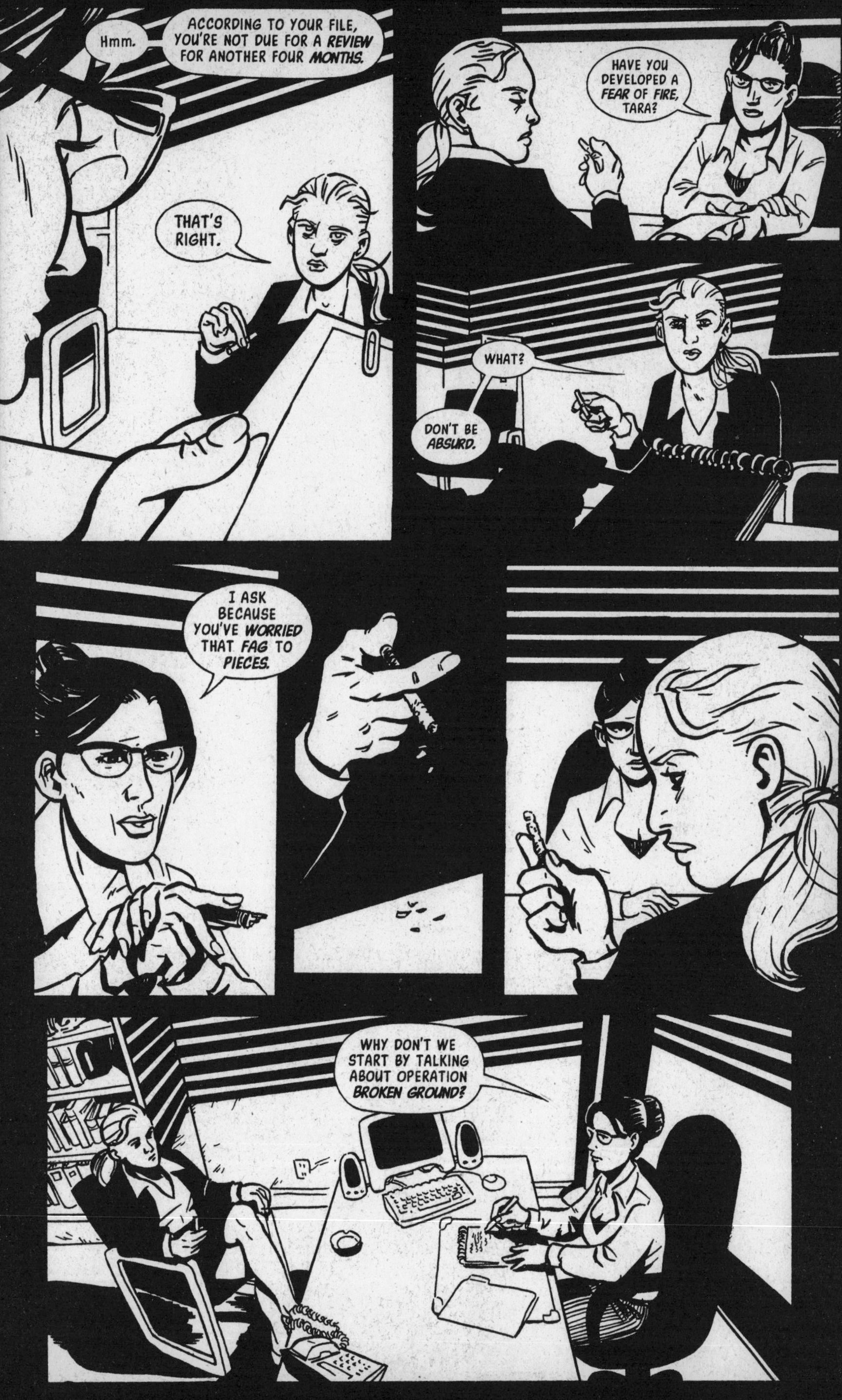

Hmm.
ACCORDING TO YOUR FILE, YOU'RE NOT DUE FOR A REVIEW FOR ANOTHER FOUR MONTHS.
THAT'S RIGHT.
HAVE YOU DEVELOPED A FEAR OF FIRE, TARA?
WHAT?
DON'T BE ABSURD.
I ASK BECAUSE YOU'VE WORRIED THAT FAG TO PIECES.
WHY DON'T WE START BY TALKING ABOUT OPERATION BROKEN GROUND?

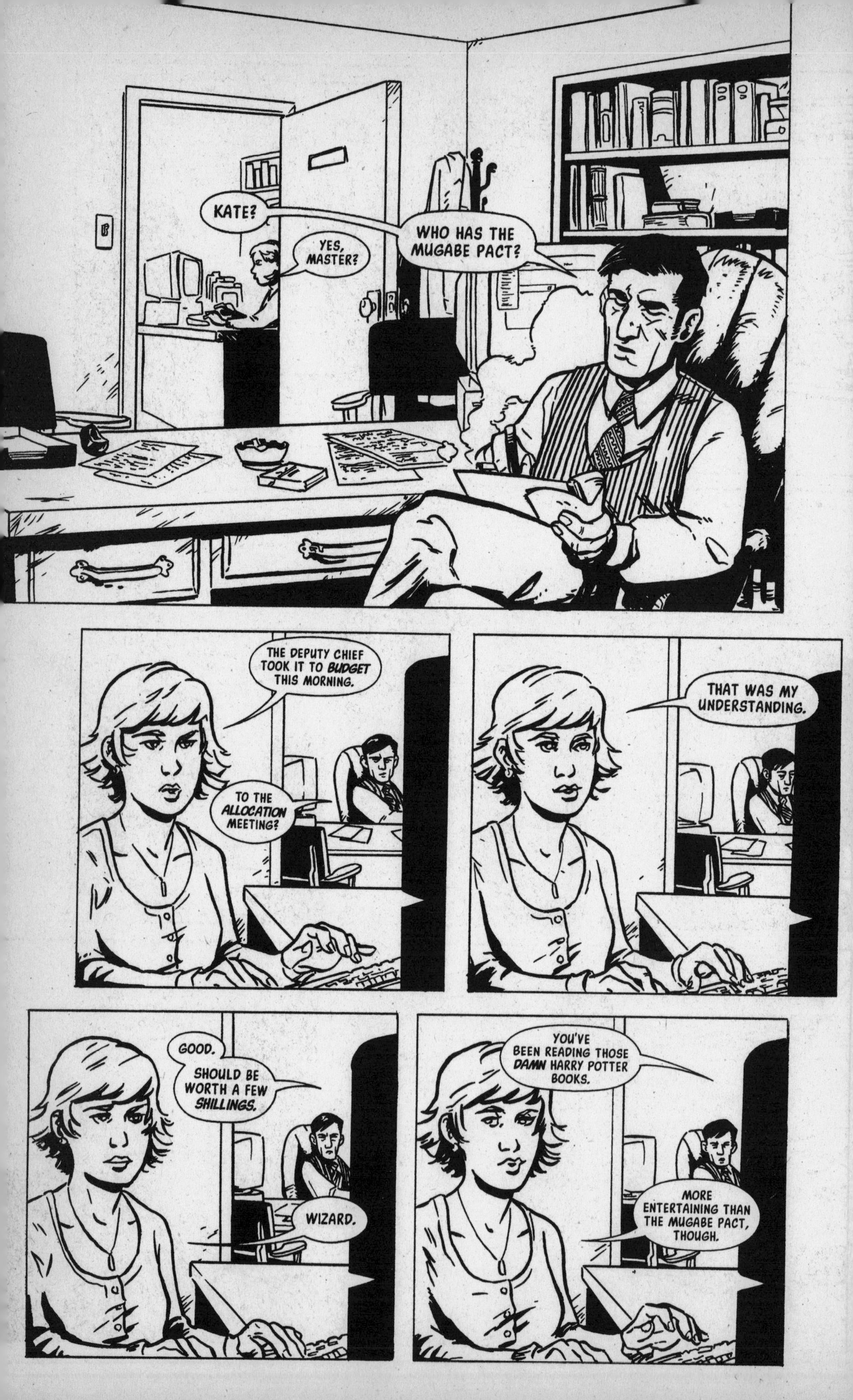
KATE?
YES, MASTER?
WHO HAS THE MUGABE PACT?
THE DEPUTY CHIEF TOOK IT TO *BUDGET* THIS MORNING.
TO THE *ALLOCATION* MEETING?
THAT WAS MY UNDERSTANDING.
GOOD.
SHOULD BE WORTH A FEW *SHILLINGS.*
WIZARD.
YOU'VE BEEN READING THOSE *DAMN* HARRY POTTER BOOKS.
MORE ENTERTAINING THAN THE MUGABE PACT, THOUGH.

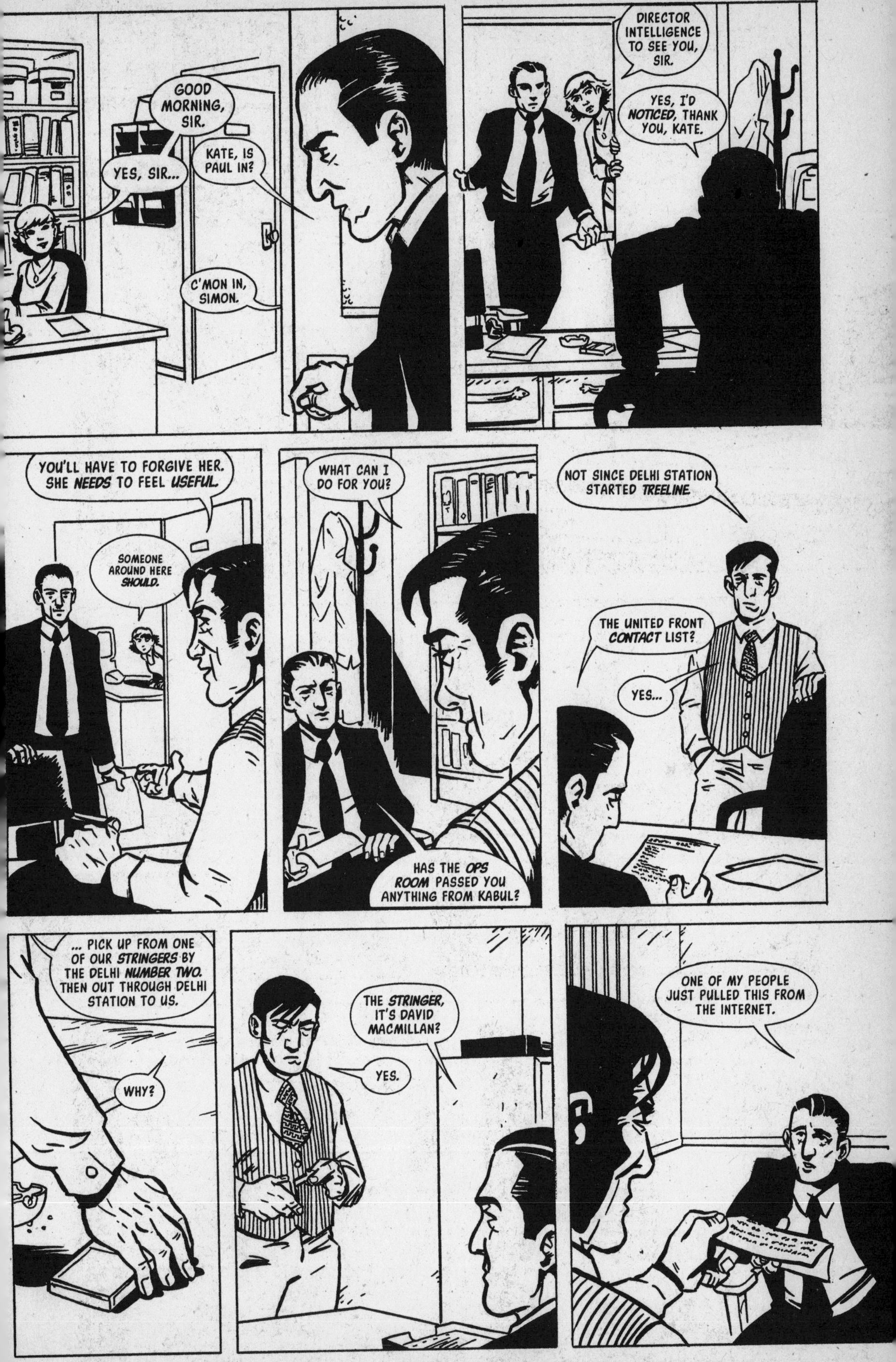
GOOD MORNING, SIR.
YES, SIR...
KATE, IS PAUL IN?
C'MON IN, SIMON.
DIRECTOR INTELLIGENCE TO SEE YOU, SIR.
YES, I'D NOTICED, THANK YOU, KATE.
YOU'LL HAVE TO FORGIVE HER. SHE NEEDS TO FEEL USEFUL.
SOMEONE AROUND HERE SHOULD.
WHAT CAN I DO FOR YOU?
HAS THE OPS ROOM PASSED YOU ANYTHING FROM KABUL?
NOT SINCE DELHI STATION STARTED TREELINE.
THE UNITED FRONT CONTACT LIST?
YES...
... PICK UP FROM ONE OF OUR STRINGERS BY THE DELHI NUMBER TWO. THEN OUT THROUGH DELHI STATION TO US.
WHY?
THE STRINGER, IT'S DAVID MACMILLAN?
YES.
ONE OF MY PEOPLE JUST PULLED THIS FROM THE INTERNET.

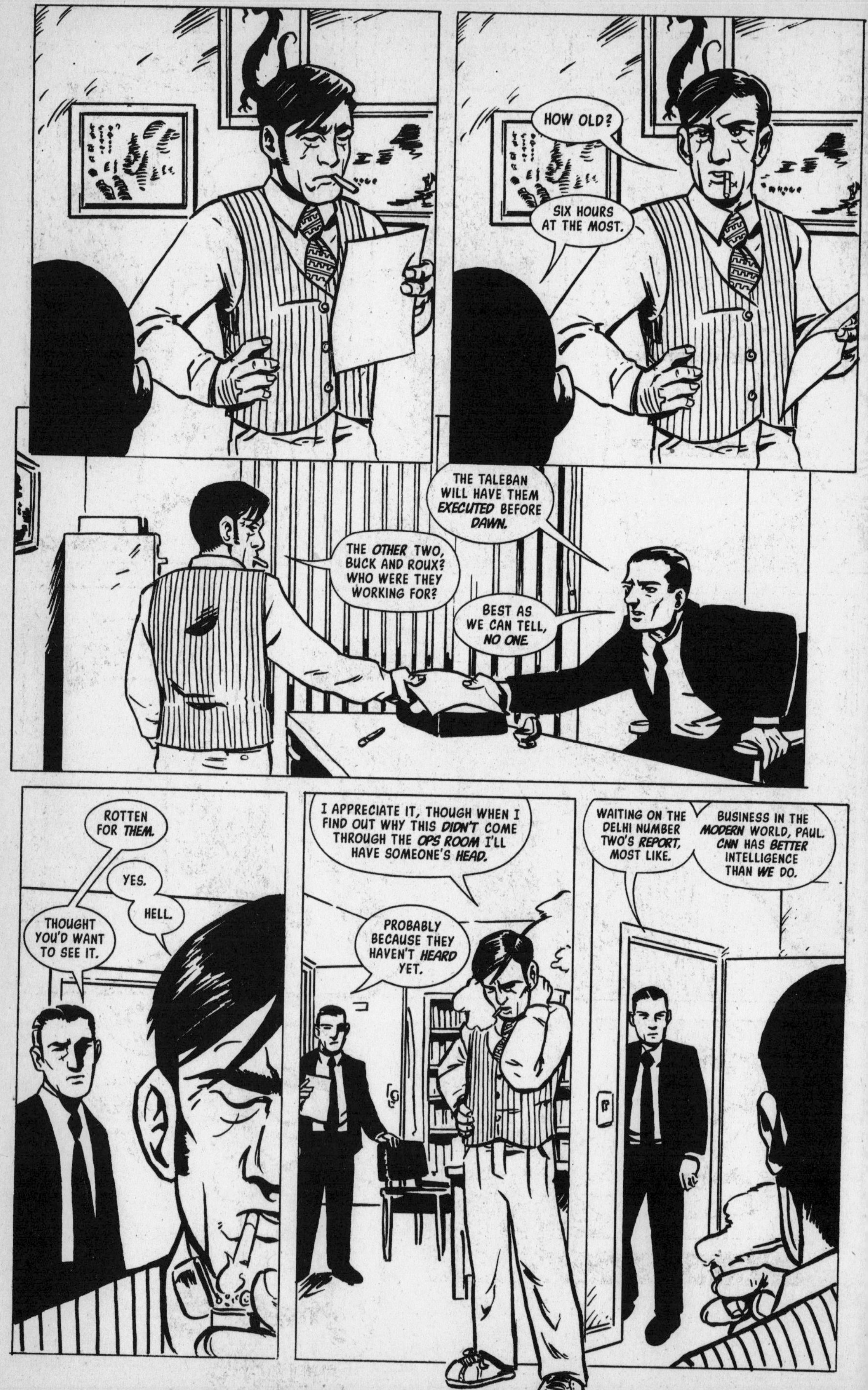
HOW OLD?
SIX HOURS AT THE MOST.
THE OTHER TWO, BUCK AND ROUX? WHO WERE THEY WORKING FOR?
THE TALEBAN WILL HAVE THEM EXECUTED BEFORE DAWN.
BEST AS WE CAN TELL, NO ONE.
THOUGHT YOU'D WANT TO SEE IT.
ROTTEN FOR THEM.
YES.
HELL.
I APPRECIATE IT, THOUGH WHEN I FIND OUT WHY THIS DIDN'T COME THROUGH THE OPS ROOM I'LL HAVE SOMEONE'S HEAD.
PROBABLY BECAUSE THEY HAVEN'T HEARD YET.
WAITING ON THE DELHI NUMBER TWO'S REPORT, MOST LIKE.
BUSINESS IN THE MODERN WORLD, PAUL. CNN HAS BETTER INTELLIGENCE THAN WE DO.

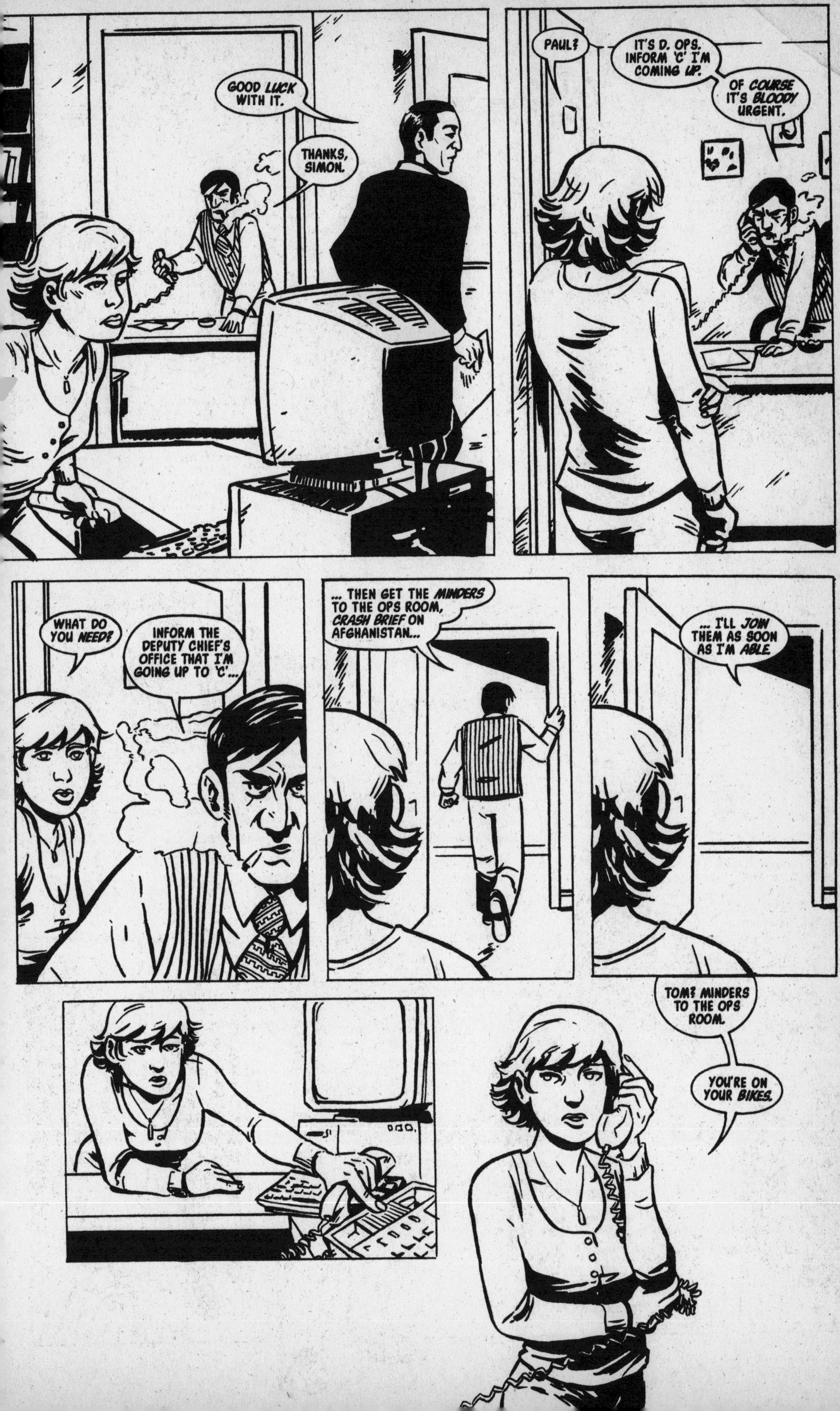

GOOD LUCK WITH IT.
THANKS, SIMON.
PAUL?
IT'S D. OPS. INFORM 'C' I'M COMING UP.
OF COURSE IT'S BLOODY URGENT.
WHAT DO YOU NEED?
INFORM THE DEPUTY CHIEF'S OFFICE THAT I'M GOING UP TO 'C'...
... THEN GET THE MINDERS TO THE OPS ROOM, CRASH BRIEF ON AFGHANISTAN...
... I'LL JOIN THEM AS SOON AS I'M ABLE.
TOM? MINDERS TO THE OPS ROOM.
YOU'RE ON YOUR BIKES.

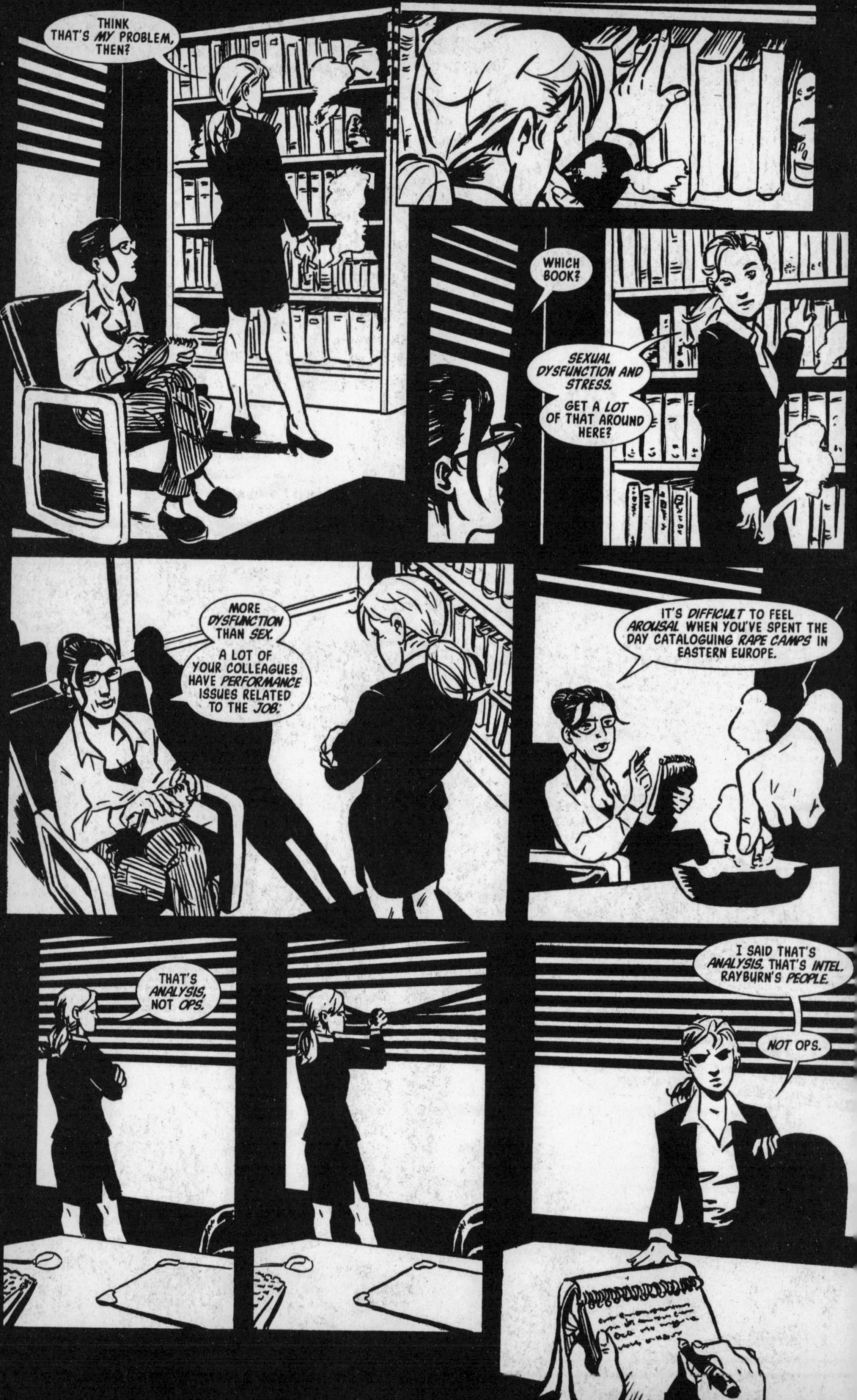
THINK THAT'S MY PROBLEM, THEN?
WHICH BOOK?
SEXUAL DYSFUNCTION AND STRESS.
GET A LOT OF THAT AROUND HERE?
MORE DYSFUNCTION THAN SEX.
A LOT OF YOUR COLLEAGUES HAVE PERFORMANCE ISSUES RELATED TO THE JOB.
IT'S DIFFICULT TO FEEL AROUSAL WHEN YOU'VE SPENT THE DAY CATALOGUING RAPE CAMPS IN EASTERN EUROPE.
THAT'S ANALYSIS, NOT OPS.
I SAID THAT'S ANALYSIS. THAT'S INTEL. RAYBURN'S PEOPLE.
NOT OPS.

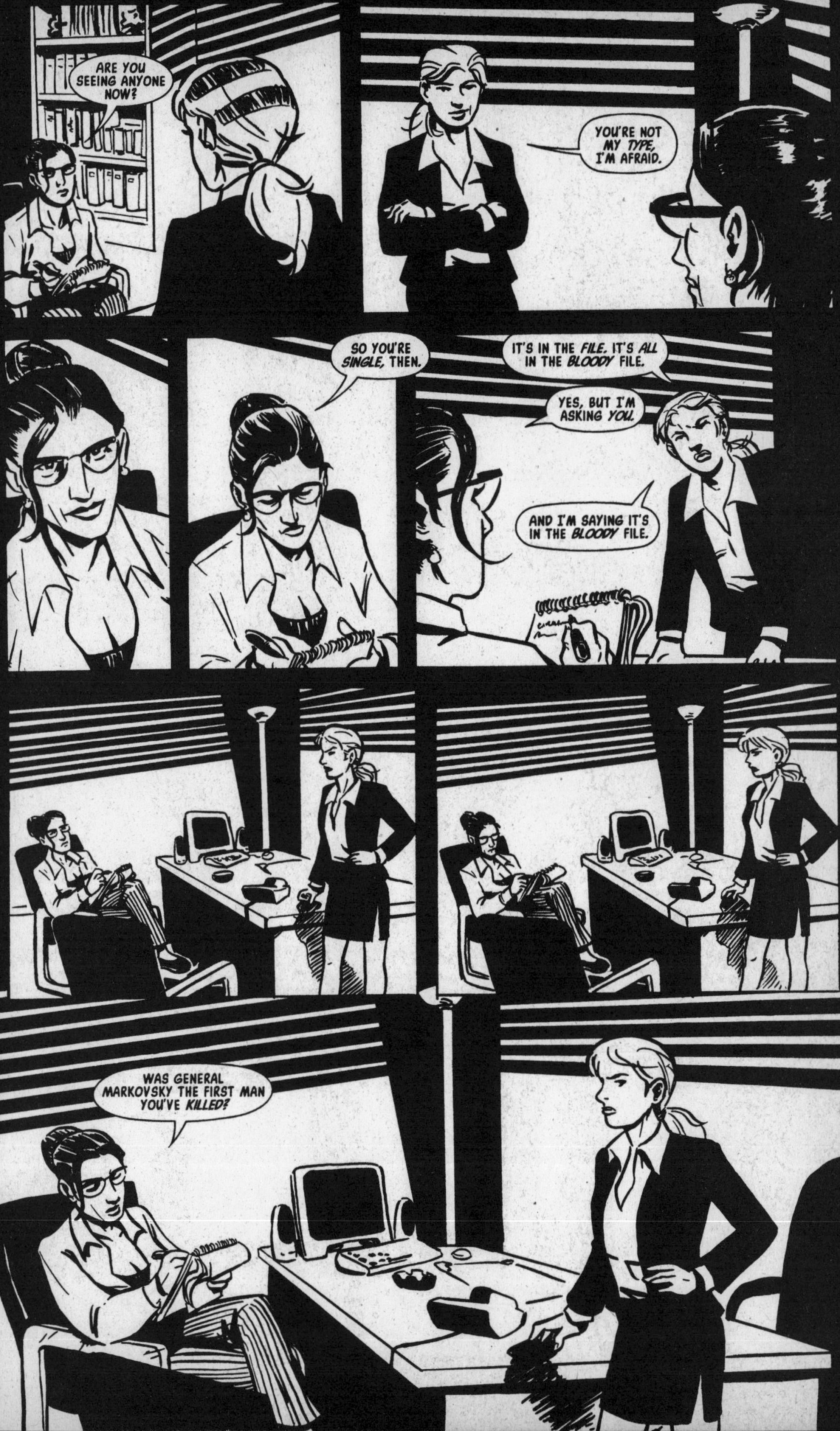
ARE YOU SEEING ANYONE NOW?
YOU'RE NOT MY TYPE, I'M AFRAID.
SO YOU'RE SINGLE, THEN.
IT'S IN THE FILE. IT'S ALL IN THE BLOODY FILE.
YES, BUT I'M ASKING YOU.
AND I'M SAYING IT'S IN THE BLOODY FILE.
WAS GENERAL MARKOVSKY THE FIRST MAN YOU'VE KILLED?

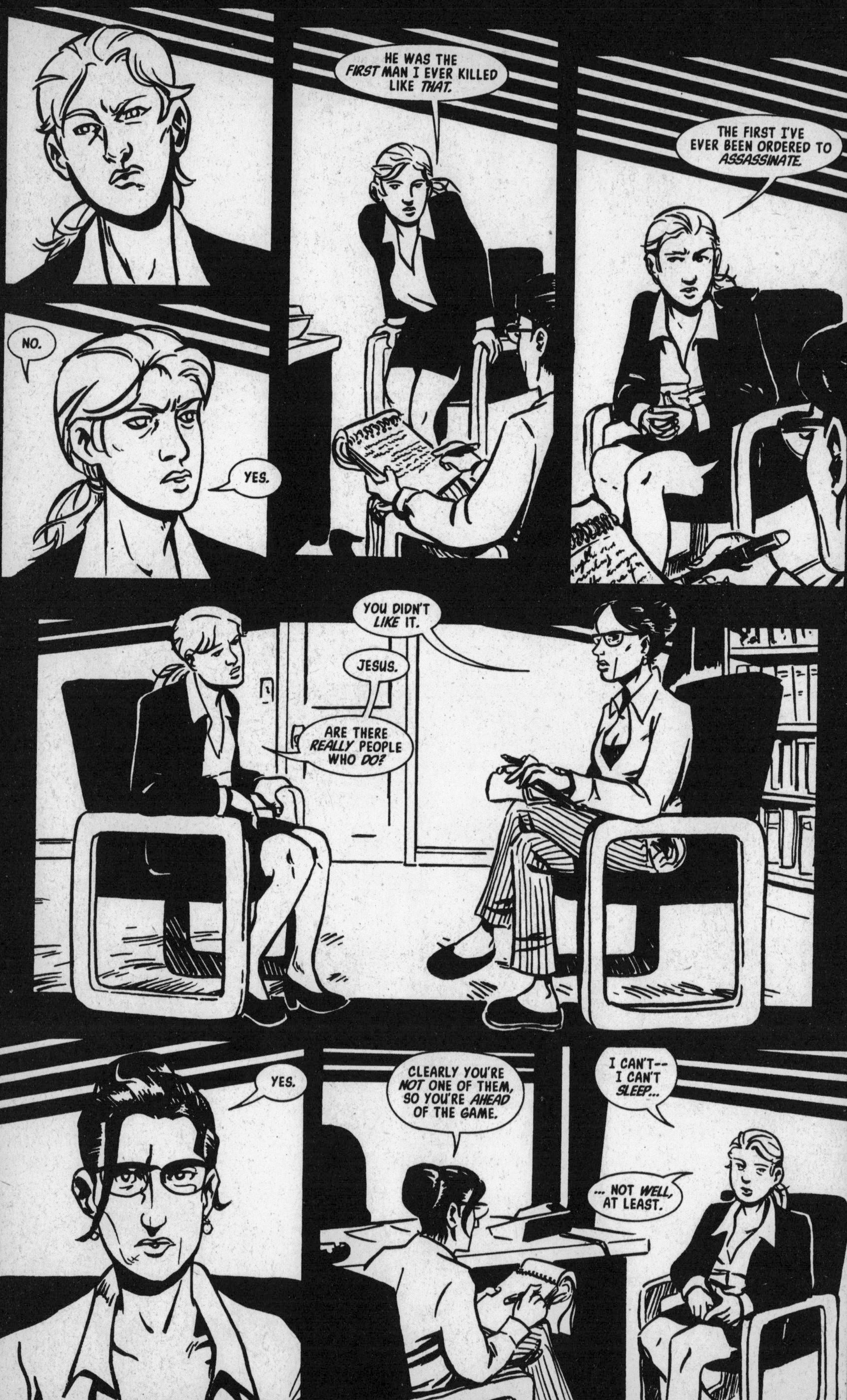
HE WAS THE *FIRST* MAN I EVER KILLED LIKE *THAT.*
THE FIRST I'VE EVER BEEN ORDERED TO *ASSASSINATE.*
NO.
YES.
YOU DIDN'T *LIKE* IT.
JESUS.
ARE THERE *REALLY* PEOPLE WHO *DO?*
YES.
CLEARLY YOU'RE *NOT* ONE OF THEM, SO YOU'RE *AHEAD* OF THE GAME.
I CAN'T-- I CAN'T *SLEEP*...
... NOT *WELL,* AT LEAST.

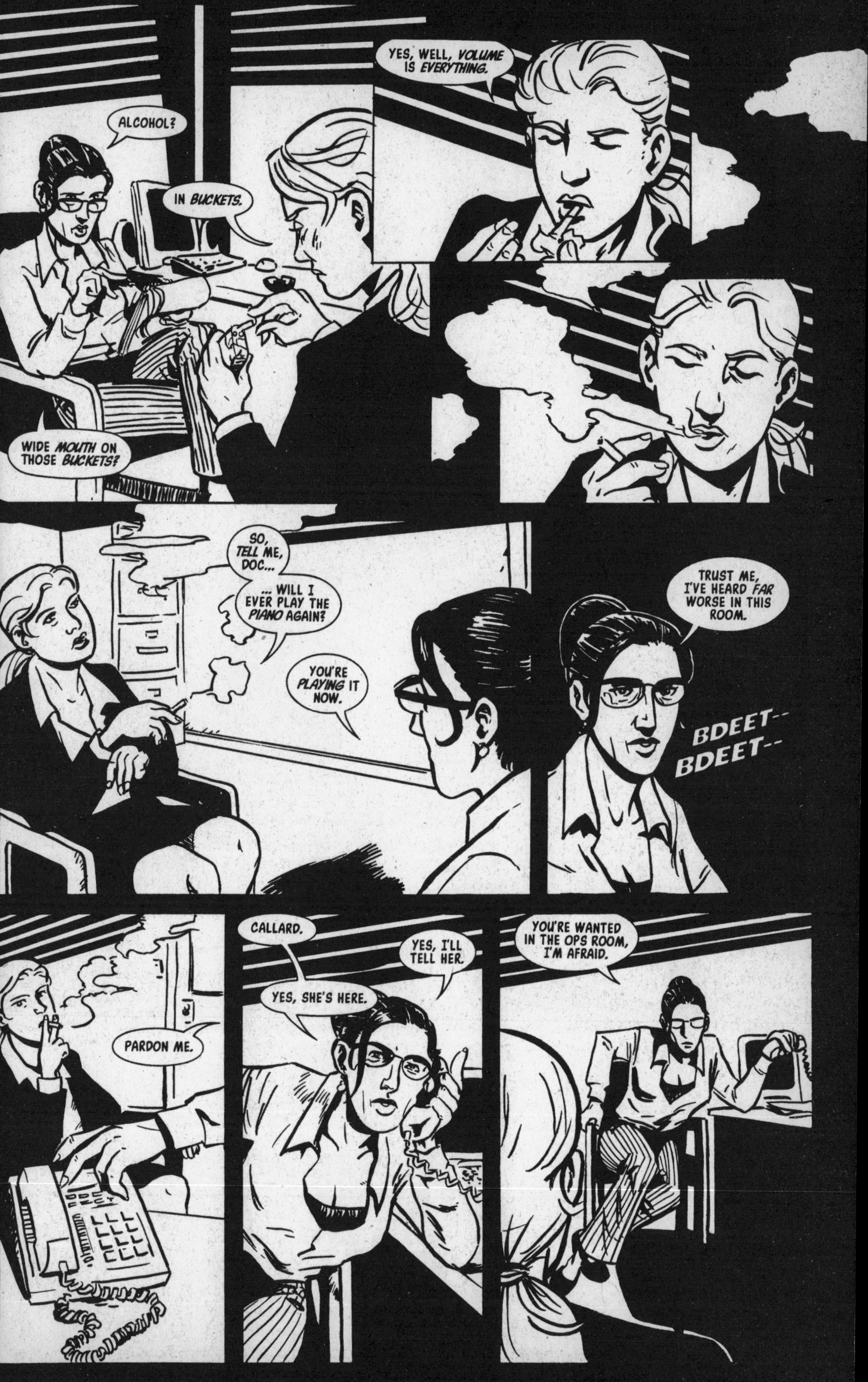
ALCOHOL?
IN BUCKETS.
WIDE MOUTH ON THOSE BUCKETS?
YES, WELL, VOLUME IS EVERYTHING.
SO, TELL ME, DOC...
... WILL I EVER PLAY THE PIANO AGAIN?
YOU'RE PLAYING IT NOW.
TRUST ME, I'VE HEARD FAR WORSE IN THIS ROOM.
BDEET-- BDEET--
PARDON ME.
CALLARD.
YES, SHE'S HERE.
YES, I'LL TELL HER.
YOU'RE WANTED IN THE OPS ROOM, I'M AFRAID.

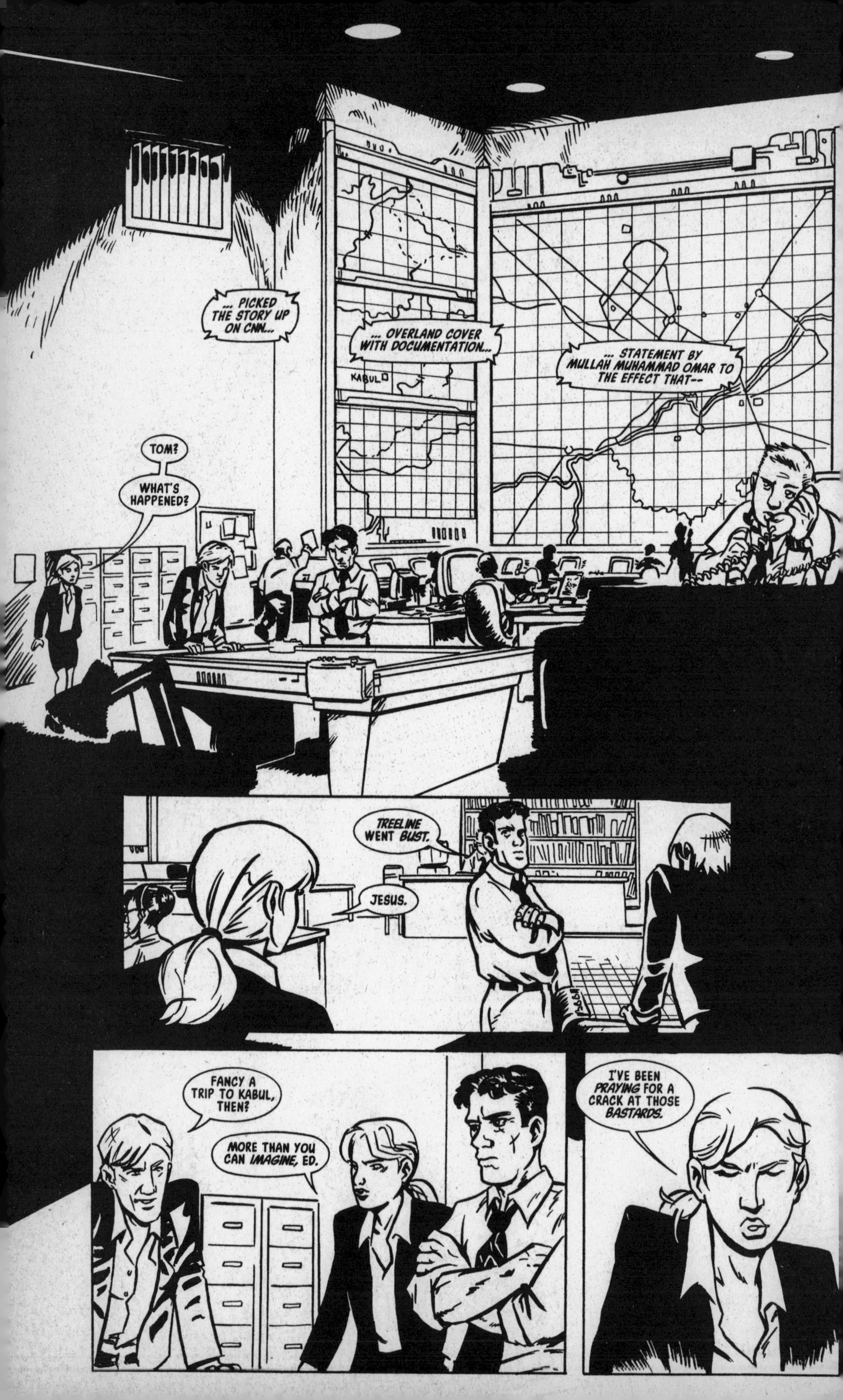
... PICKED THE STORY UP ON CNN...
... OVERLAND COVER WITH DOCUMENTATION...
KABUL
... STATEMENT BY MULLAH MUHAMMAD OMAR TO THE EFFECT THAT--
TOM?
WHAT'S HAPPENED?
TREELINE WENT *BUST.*
JESUS.
FANCY A TRIP TO KABUL, THEN?
MORE THAN YOU CAN *IMAGINE,* ED.
I'VE BEEN *PRAYING* FOR A CRACK AT THOSE *BASTARDS.*

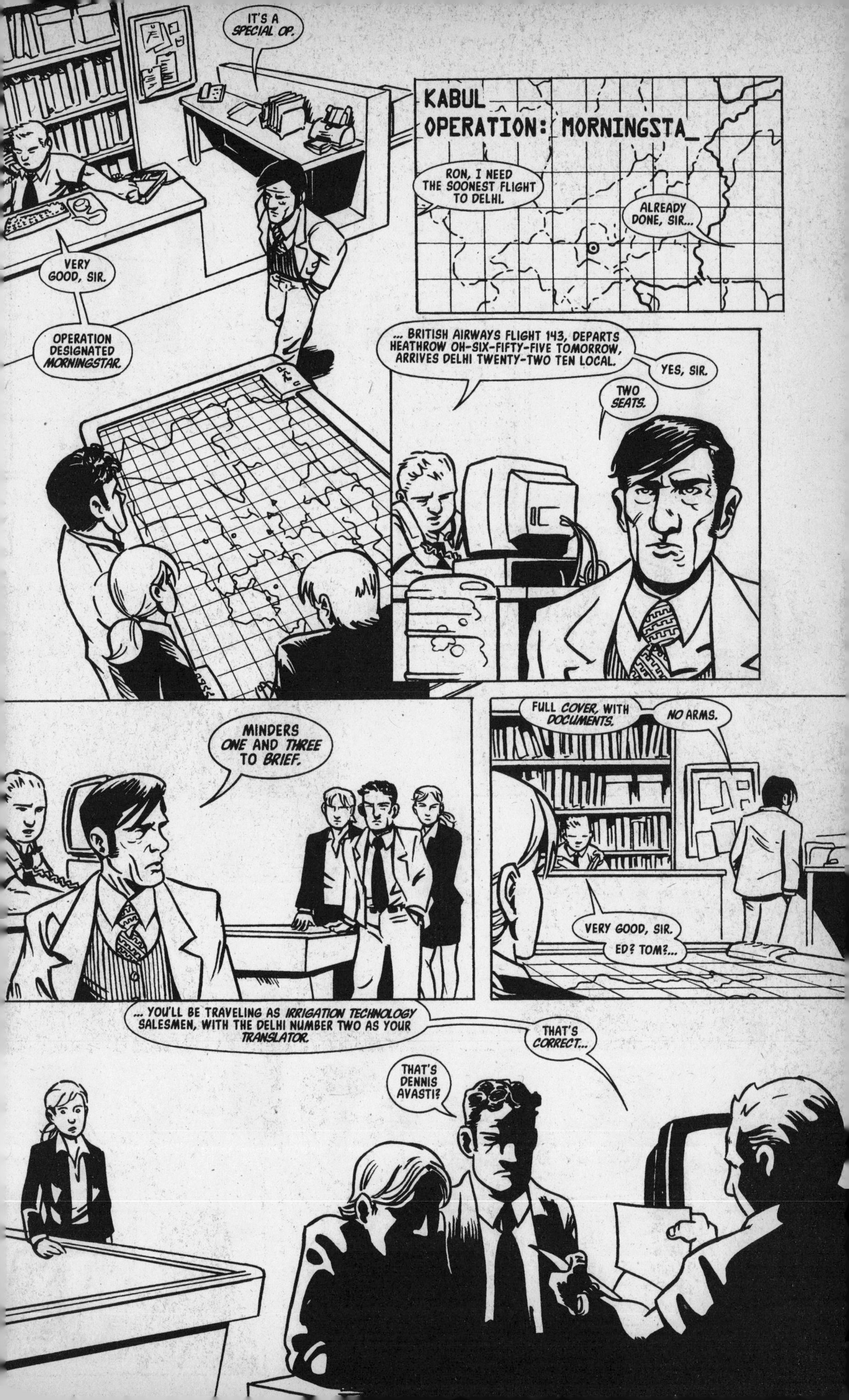
IT'S A SPECIAL OP.
VERY GOOD, SIR.
OPERATION DESIGNATED MORNINGSTAR.
KABUL
OPERATION: MORNINGSTA_
RON, I NEED THE SOONEST FLIGHT TO DELHI.
ALREADY DONE, SIR...
... BRITISH AIRWAYS FLIGHT 143, DEPARTS HEATHROW OH-SIX-FIFTY-FIVE TOMORROW, ARRIVES DELHI TWENTY-TWO TEN LOCAL.
YES, SIR.
TWO SEATS.
MINDERS ONE AND THREE TO BRIEF.
FULL COVER, WITH DOCUMENTS.
NO ARMS.
VERY GOOD, SIR.
ED? TOM?...
... YOU'LL BE TRAVELING AS IRRIGATION TECHNOLOGY SALESMEN, WITH THE DELHI NUMBER TWO AS YOUR TRANSLATOR.
THAT'S CORRECT...
THAT'S DENNIS AVASTI?

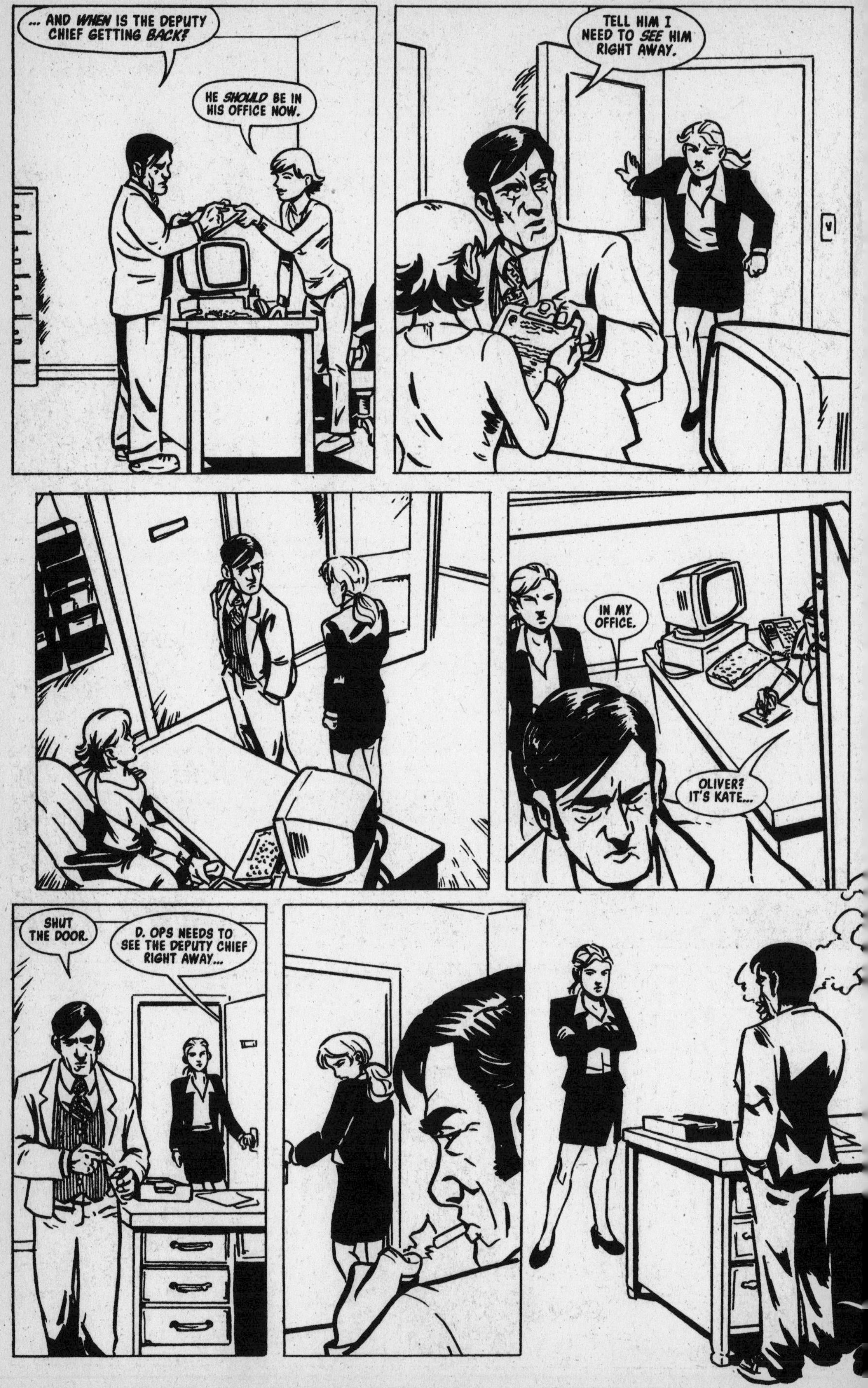
... AND WHEN IS THE DEPUTY CHIEF GETTING BACK?
HE SHOULD BE IN HIS OFFICE NOW.
TELL HIM I NEED TO SEE HIM RIGHT AWAY.
IN MY OFFICE.
OLIVER? IT'S KATE...
SHUT THE DOOR.
D. OPS NEEDS TO SEE THE DEPUTY CHIEF RIGHT AWAY...

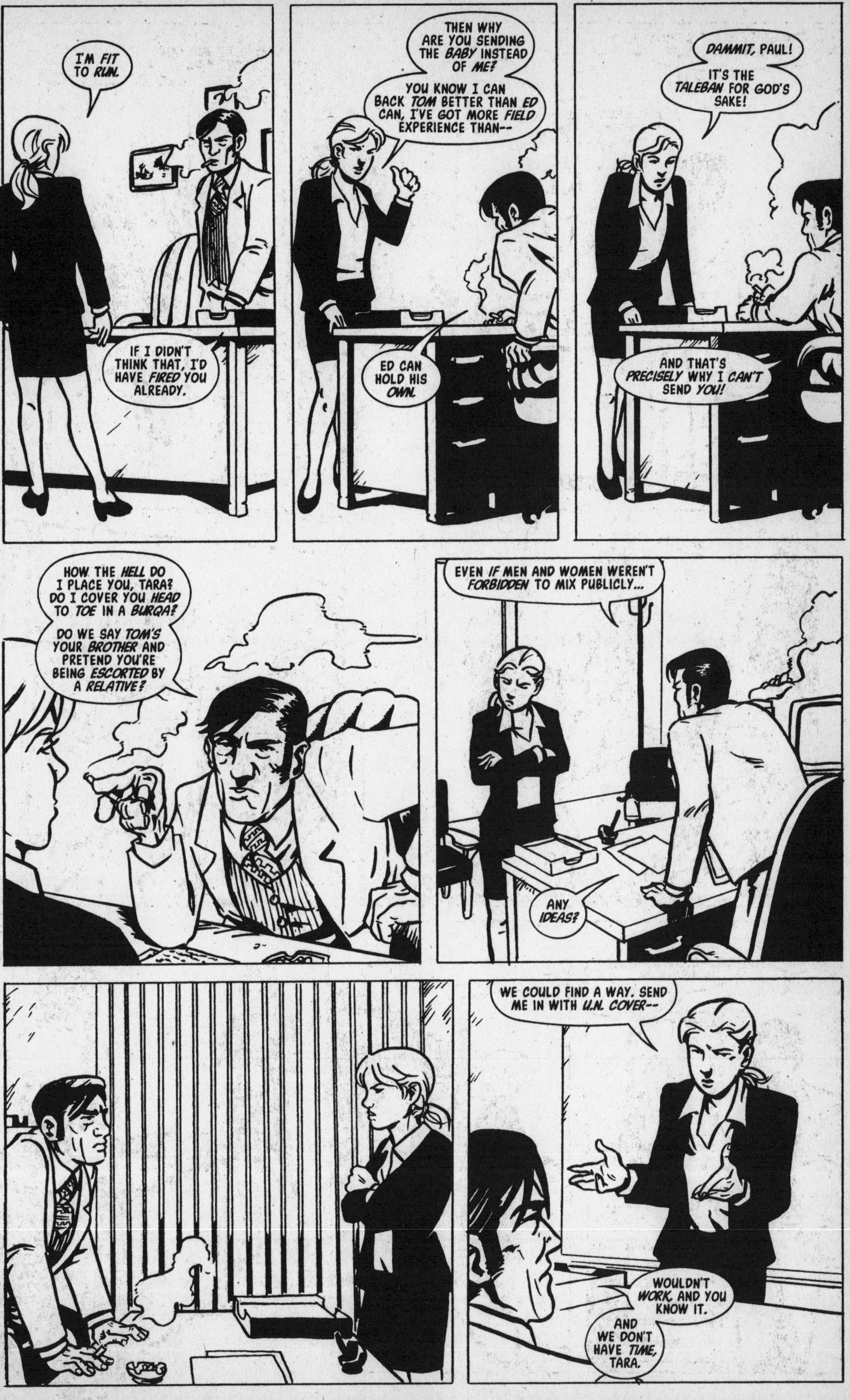
I'M FIT TO RUN.
IF I DIDN'T THINK THAT, I'D HAVE FIRED YOU ALREADY.
THEN WHY ARE YOU SENDING THE BABY INSTEAD OF ME?
YOU KNOW I CAN BACK TOM BETTER THAN ED CAN, I'VE GOT MORE FIELD EXPERIENCE THAN--
ED CAN HOLD HIS OWN.
DAMMIT, PAUL!
IT'S THE TALEBAN FOR GOD'S SAKE!
AND THAT'S PRECISELY WHY I CAN'T SEND YOU!
HOW THE HELL DO I PLACE YOU, TARA? DO I COVER YOU HEAD TO TOE IN A BURQA?
DO WE SAY TOM'S YOUR BROTHER AND PRETEND YOU'RE BEING ESCORTED BY A RELATIVE?
EVEN IF MEN AND WOMEN WEREN'T FORBIDDEN TO MIX PUBLICLY...
ANY IDEAS?
WE COULD FIND A WAY. SEND ME IN WITH U.N. COVER--
WOULDN'T WORK, AND YOU KNOW IT.
AND WE DON'T HAVE TIME, TARA.

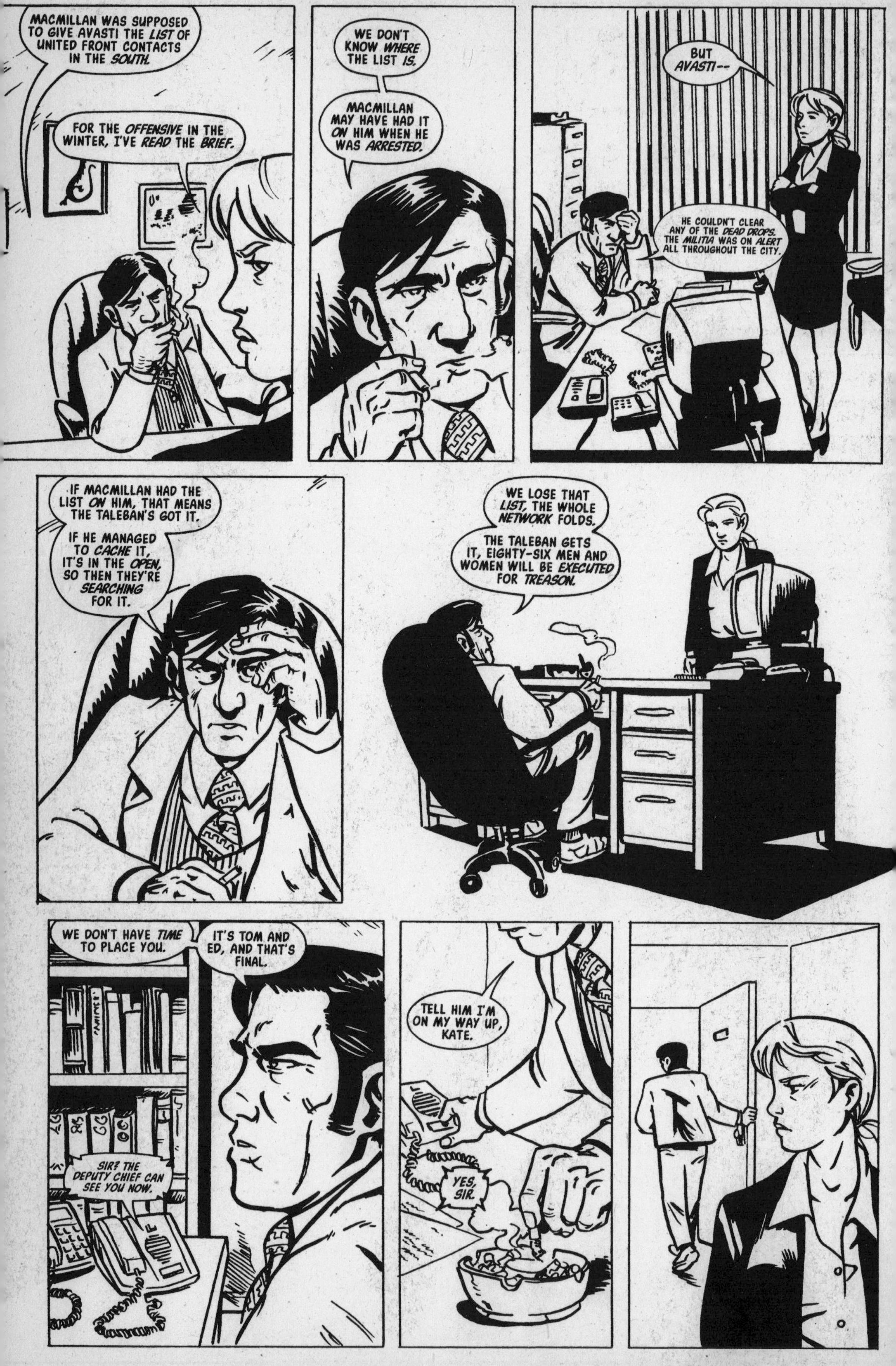
MACMILLAN WAS SUPPOSED TO GIVE AVASTI THE LIST OF UNITED FRONT CONTACTS IN THE SOUTH.
FOR THE OFFENSIVE IN THE WINTER, I'VE READ THE BRIEF.
WE DON'T KNOW WHERE THE LIST IS.
MACMILLAN MAY HAVE HAD IT ON HIM WHEN HE WAS ARRESTED.
BUT AVASTI--
HE COULDN'T CLEAR ANY OF THE DEAD DROPS. THE MILITIA WAS ON ALERT ALL THROUGHOUT THE CITY.
IF MACMILLAN HAD THE LIST ON HIM, THAT MEANS THE TALEBAN'S GOT IT.
IF HE MANAGED TO CACHE IT, IT'S IN THE OPEN, SO THEN THEY'RE SEARCHING FOR IT.
WE LOSE THAT LIST, THE WHOLE NETWORK FOLDS.
THE TALEBAN GETS IT, EIGHTY-SIX MEN AND WOMEN WILL BE EXECUTED FOR TREASON.
WE DON'T HAVE TIME TO PLACE YOU.
IT'S TOM AND ED, AND THAT'S FINAL.
SIR? THE DEPUTY CHIEF CAN SEE YOU NOW.
TELL HIM I'M ON MY WAY UP, KATE.
YES, SIR.

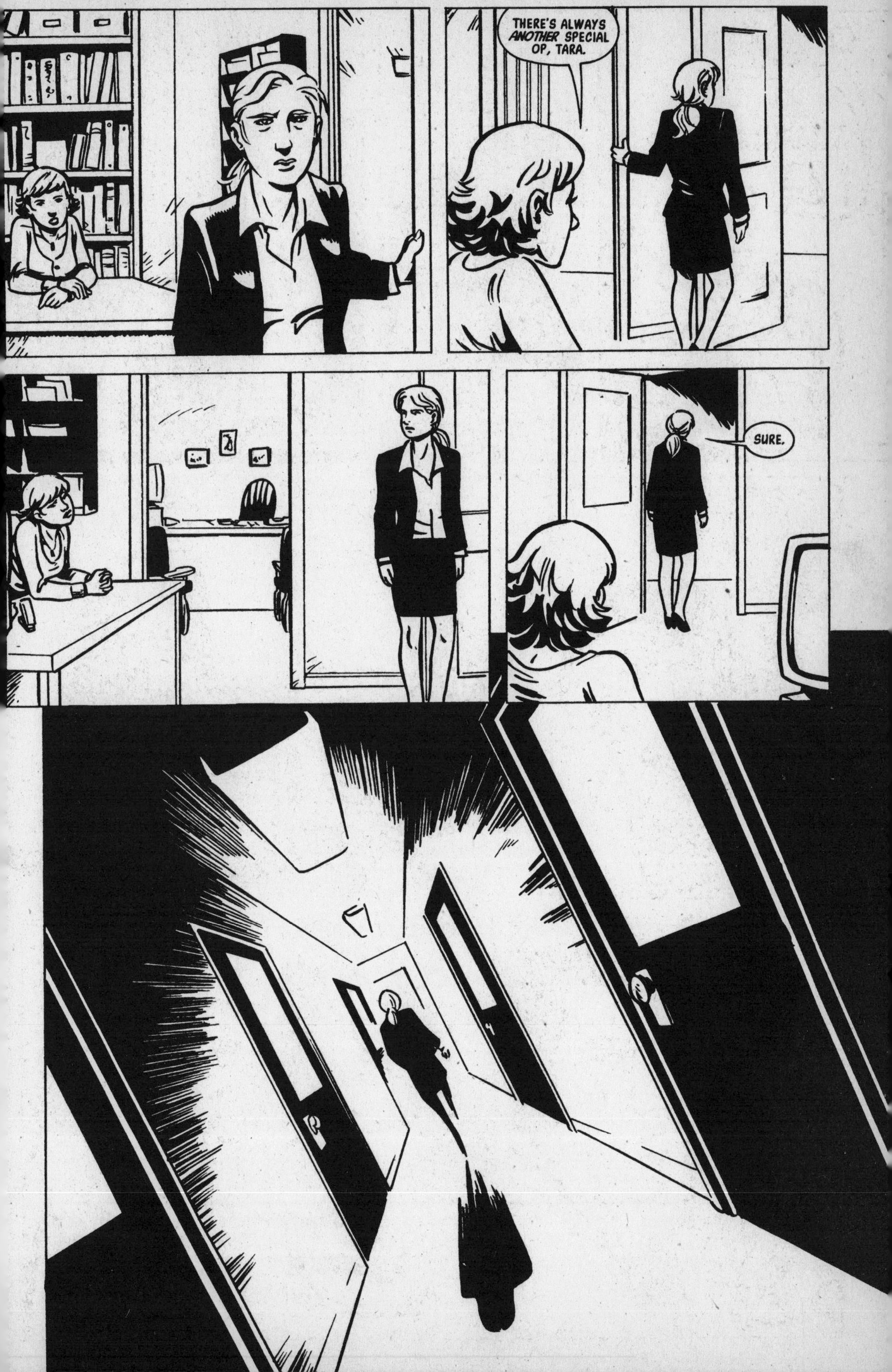
THERE'S ALWAYS ANOTHER SPECIAL OP, TARA.
SURE.

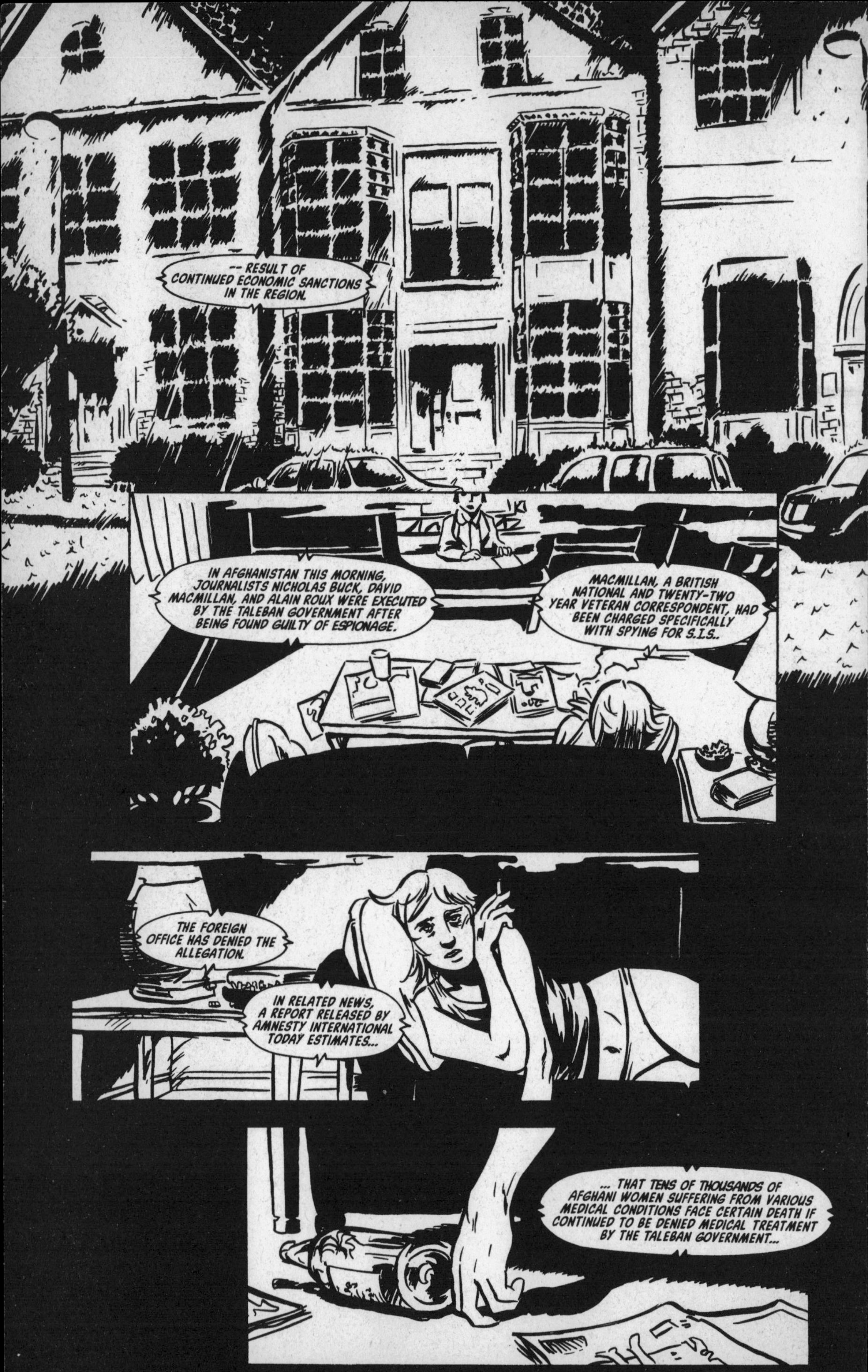
-- RESULT OF CONTINUED ECONOMIC SANCTIONS IN THE REGION.
IN AFGHANISTAN THIS MORNING, JOURNALISTS NICHOLAS BUCK, DAVID MACMILLAN, AND ALAIN ROUX WERE EXECUTED BY THE TALEBAN GOVERNMENT AFTER BEING FOUND GUILTY OF ESPIONAGE.
MACMILLAN, A BRITISH NATIONAL AND TWENTY-TWO YEAR VETERAN CORRESPONDENT, HAD BEEN CHARGED SPECIFICALLY WITH SPYING FOR S.I.S..
THE FOREIGN OFFICE HAS DENIED THE ALLEGATION.
IN RELATED NEWS, A REPORT RELEASED BY AMNESTY INTERNATIONAL TODAY ESTIMATES...
... THAT TENS OF THOUSANDS OF AFGHANI WOMEN SUFFERING FROM VARIOUS MEDICAL CONDITIONS FACE CERTAIN DEATH IF CONTINUED TO BE DENIED MEDICAL TREATMENT BY THE TALEBAN GOVERNMENT...

CHAPTER 2

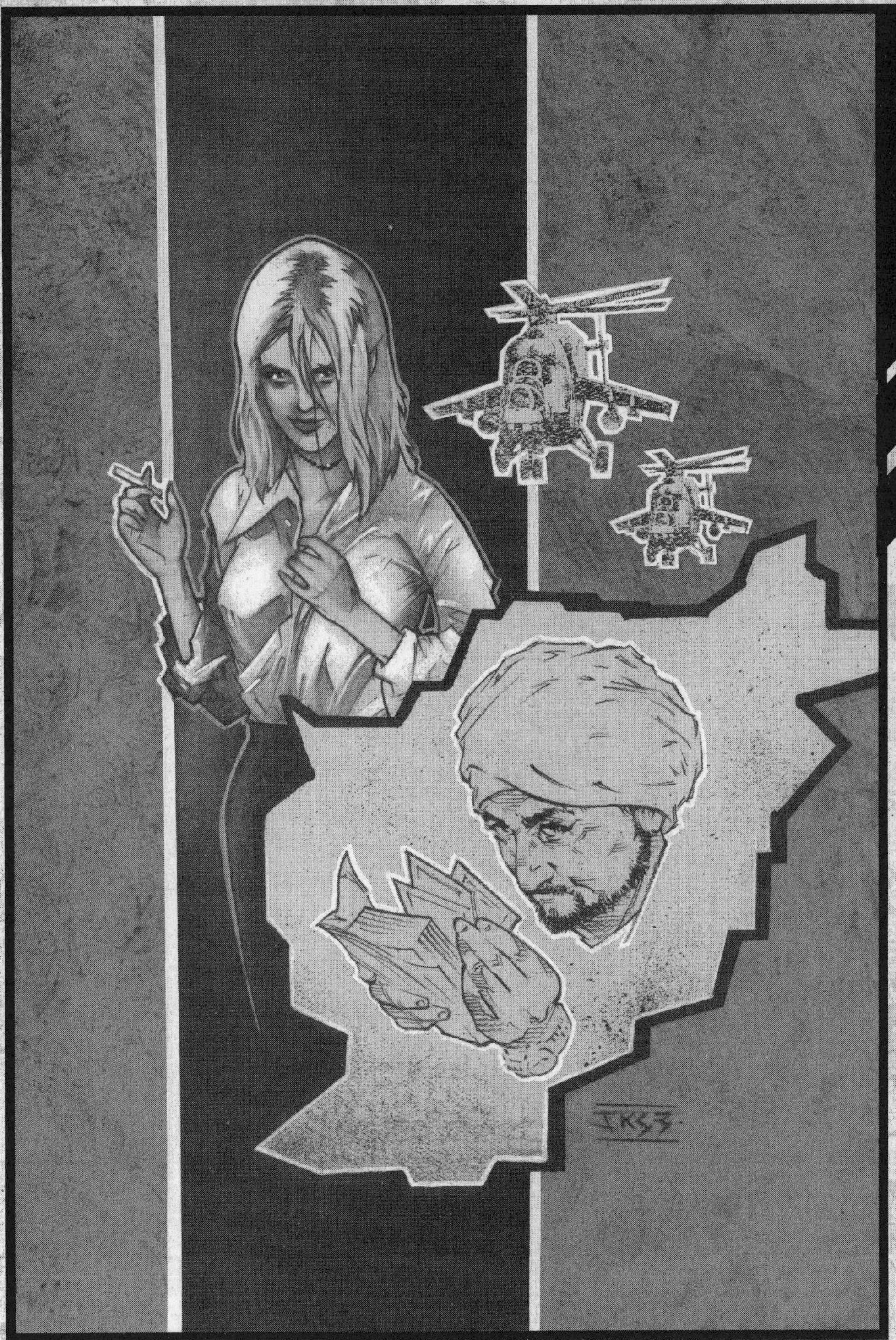

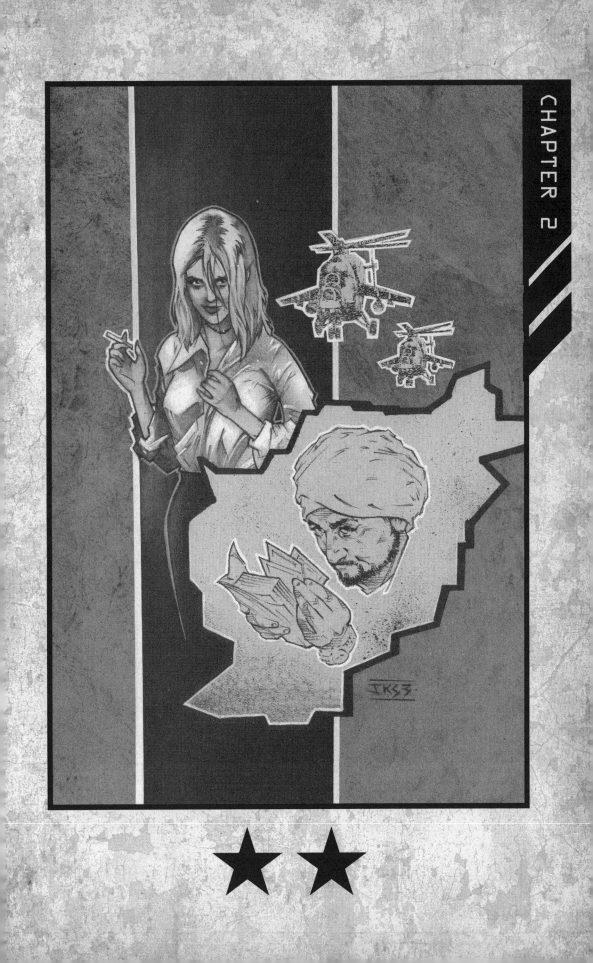

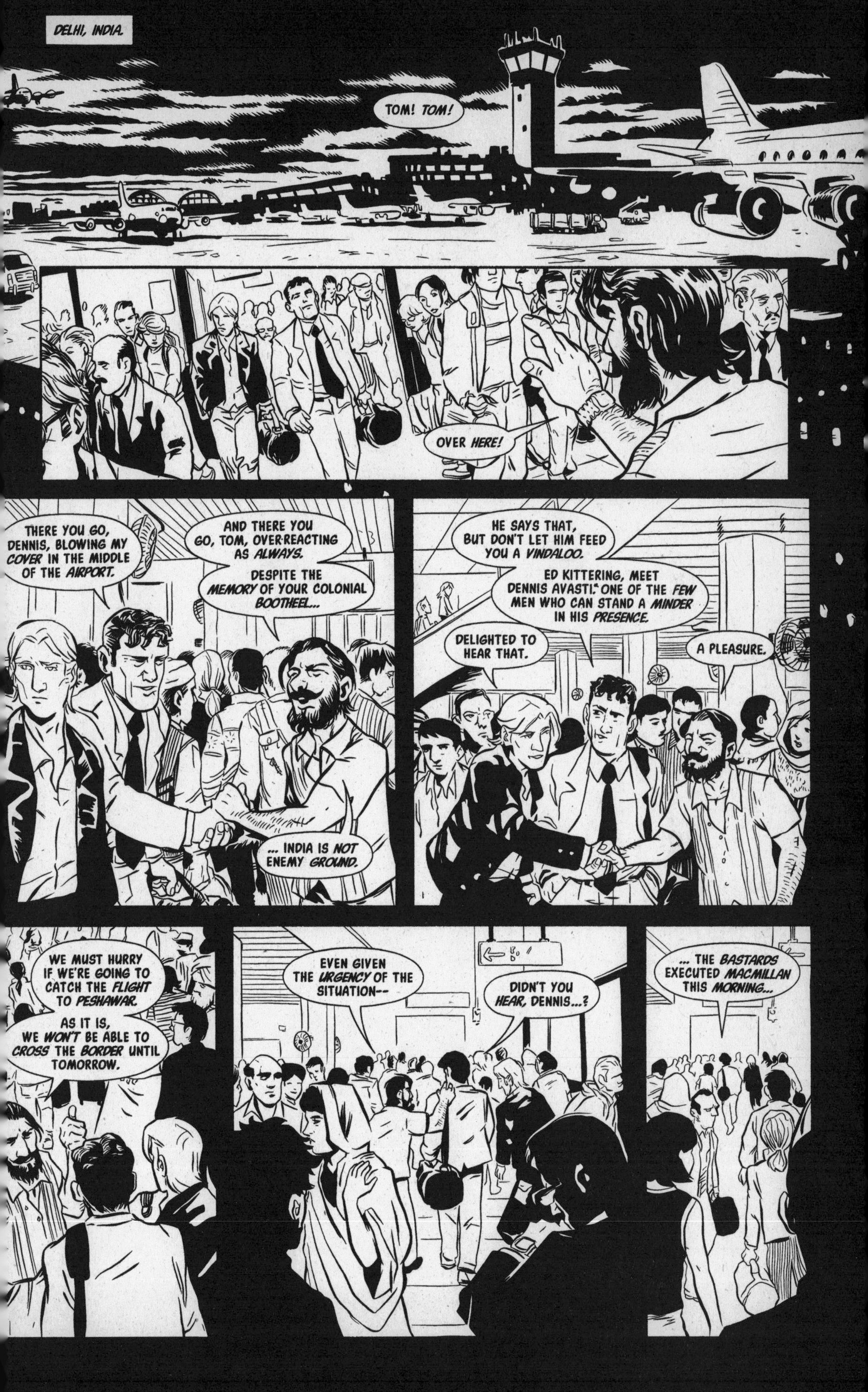
DELHI, INDIA.
TOM! TOM!
OVER HERE!
THERE YOU GO, DENNIS, BLOWING MY COVER IN THE MIDDLE OF THE AIRPORT.
AND THERE YOU GO, TOM, OVER-REACTING AS ALWAYS.
DESPITE THE MEMORY OF YOUR COLONIAL BOOTHEEL...
... INDIA IS NOT ENEMY GROUND.
HE SAYS THAT, BUT DON'T LET HIM FEED YOU A VINDALOO.
ED KITTERING, MEET DENNIS AVASTI. ONE OF THE FEW MEN WHO CAN STAND A MINDER IN HIS PRESENCE.
DELIGHTED TO HEAR THAT.
A PLEASURE.
WE MUST HURRY IF WE'RE GOING TO CATCH THE FLIGHT TO PESHAWAR.
AS IT IS, WE WON'T BE ABLE TO CROSS THE BORDER UNTIL TOMORROW.
EVEN GIVEN THE URGENCY OF THE SITUATION--
DIDN'T YOU HEAR, DENNIS...?
... THE BASTARDS EXECUTED MACMILLAN THIS MORNING...

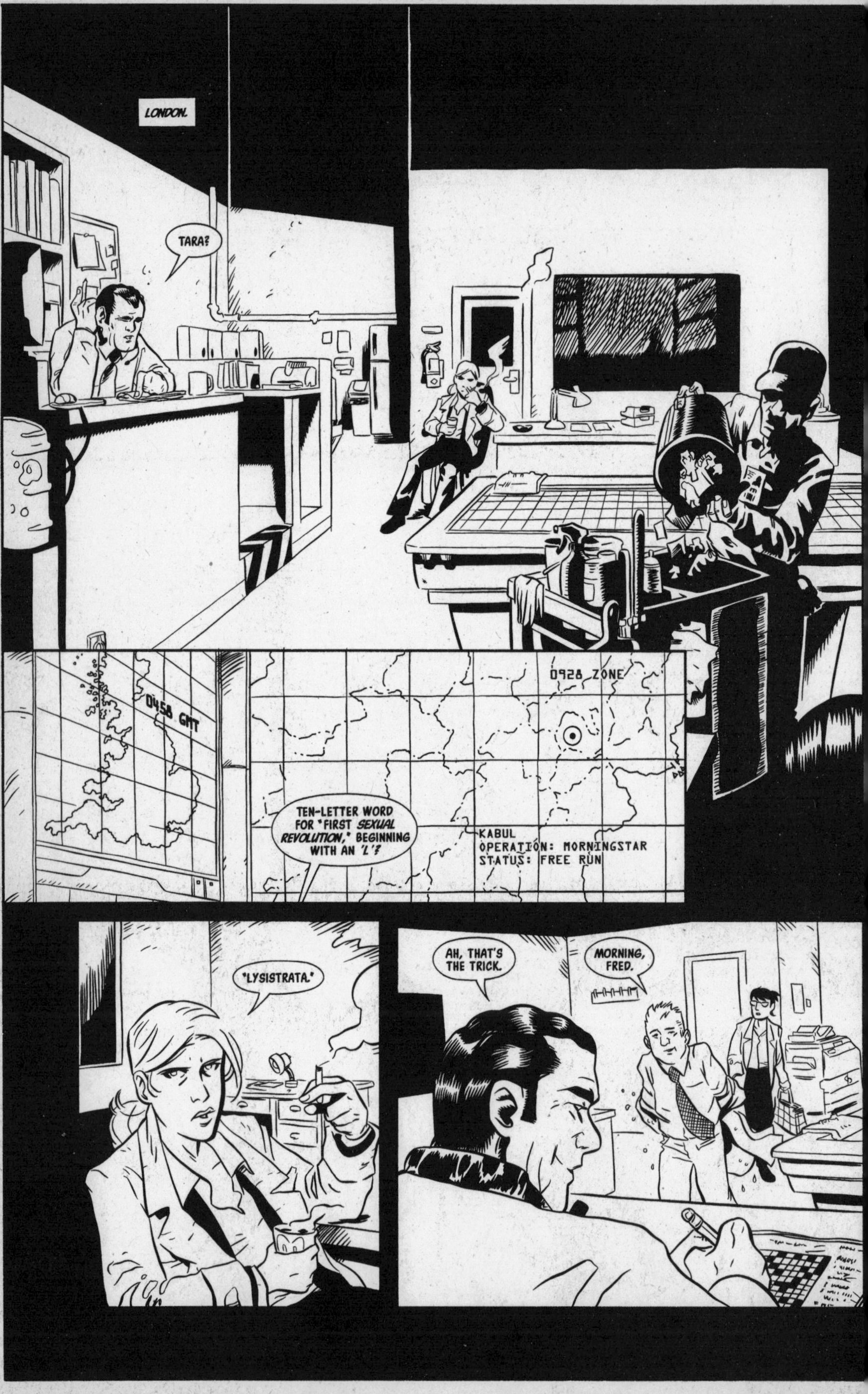
LONDON.
TARA?
0458 GMT
0928 ZONE
TEN-LETTER WORD FOR "FIRST *SEXUAL REVOLUTION*," BEGINNING WITH AN 'L'?
KABUL
OPERATION: MORNINGSTAR
STATUS: FREE RUN
"LYSISTRATA."
AH, THAT'S THE TRICK.
MORNING, FRED.

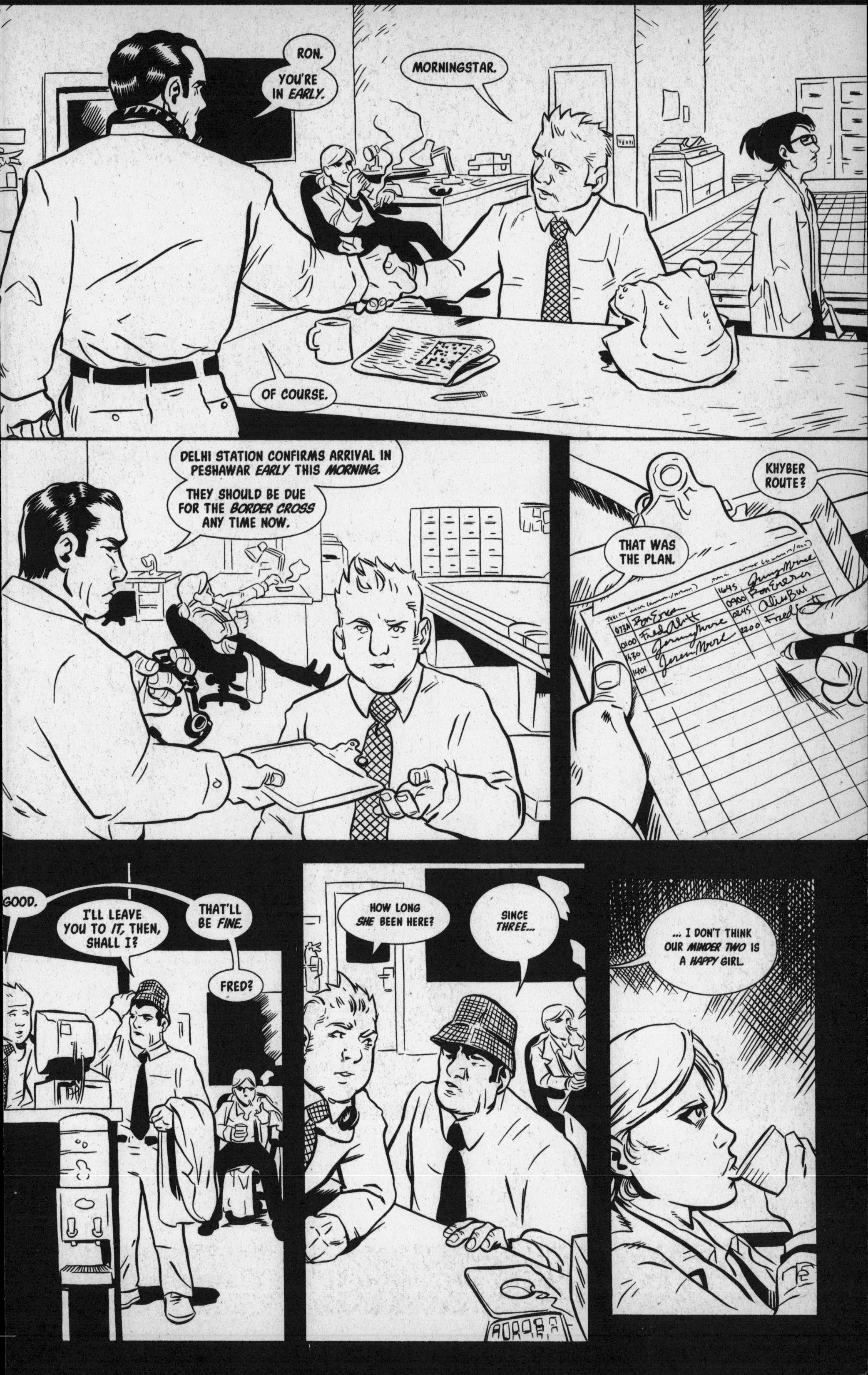
RON.
YOU'RE IN EARLY.
MORNINGSTAR.
OF COURSE.
DELHI STATION CONFIRMS ARRIVAL IN PESHAWAR EARLY THIS MORNING.
THEY SHOULD BE DUE FOR THE BORDER CROSS ANY TIME NOW.
KHYBER ROUTE?
THAT WAS THE PLAN.
GOOD.
I'LL LEAVE YOU TO IT, THEN, SHALL I?
THAT'LL BE FINE.
FRED?
HOW LONG SHE BEEN HERE?
SINCE THREE...
... I DON'T THINK OUR MINDER TWO IS A HAPPY GIRL.

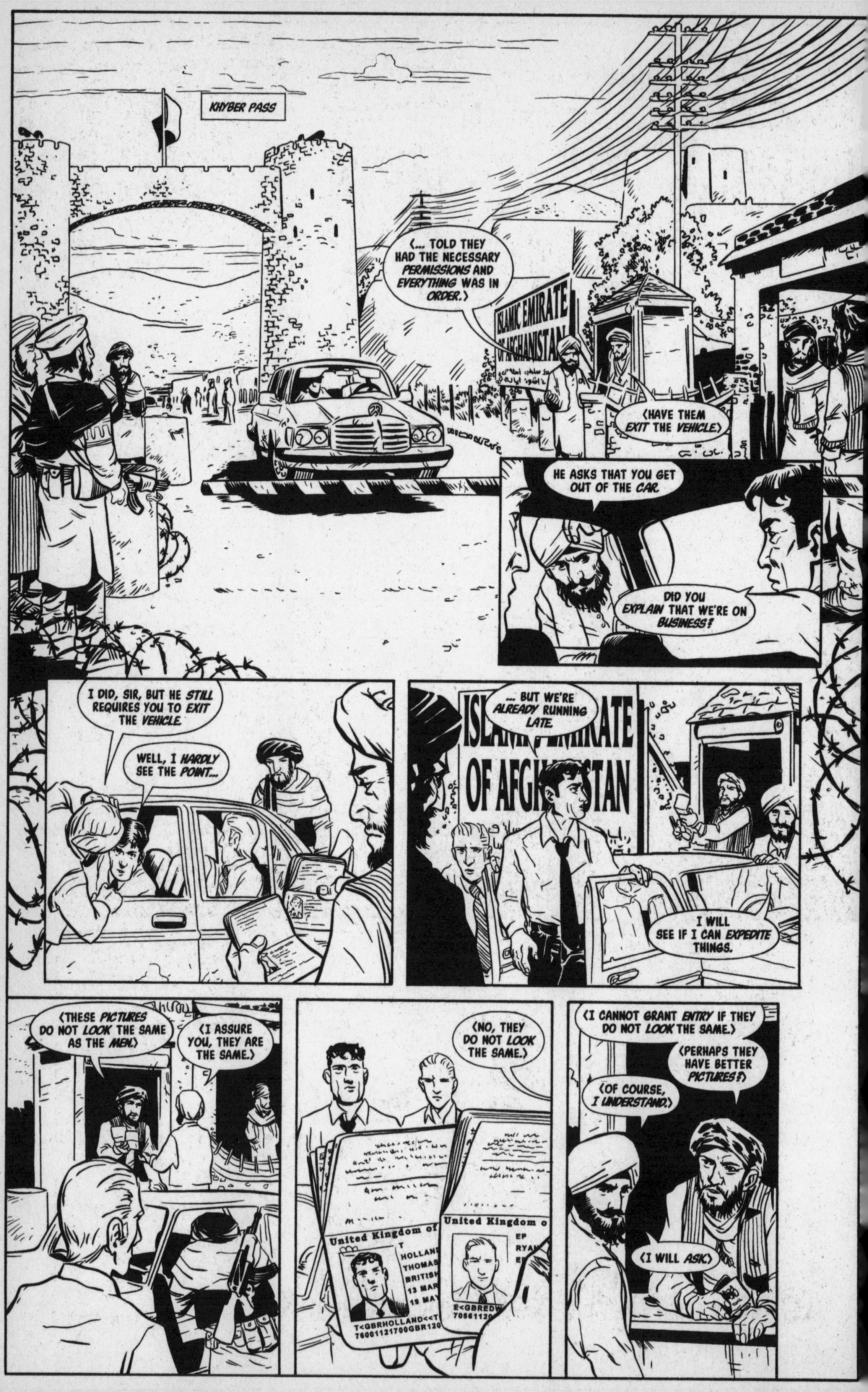
KHYBER PASS
‹... TOLD THEY HAD THE NECESSARY PERMISSIONS AND EVERYTHING WAS IN ORDER.›
ISLAMIC EMIRATE OF AFGHANISTAN
‹HAVE THEM EXIT THE VEHICLE.›
HE ASKS THAT YOU GET OUT OF THE CAR.
DID YOU EXPLAIN THAT WE'RE ON BUSINESS?
I DID, SIR, BUT HE STILL REQUIRES YOU TO EXIT THE VEHICLE.
WELL, I HARDLY SEE THE POINT...
... BUT WE'RE ALREADY RUNNING LATE.
I WILL SEE IF I CAN EXPEDITE THINGS.
‹THESE PICTURES DO NOT LOOK THE SAME AS THE MEN.›
‹I ASSURE YOU, THEY ARE THE SAME.›
‹NO, THEY DO NOT LOOK THE SAME.›
United Kingdom of
‹I CANNOT GRANT ENTRY IF THEY DO NOT LOOK THE SAME.›
‹PERHAPS THEY HAVE BETTER PICTURES?›
‹OF COURSE, I UNDERSTAND.›
‹I WILL ASK.›

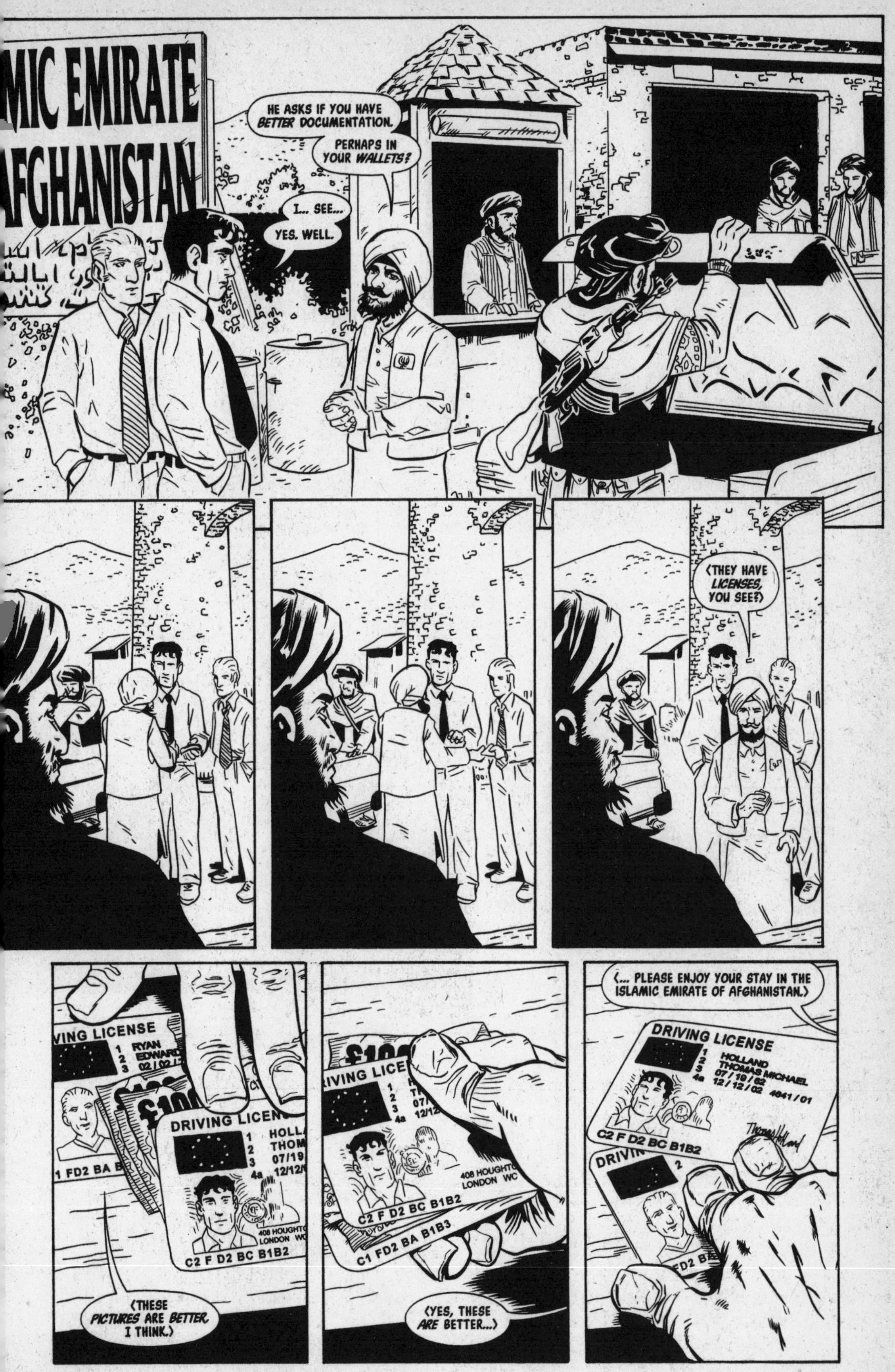
MIC EMIRATE
AFGHANISTAN
HE ASKS IF YOU HAVE BETTER DOCUMENTATION.
PERHAPS IN YOUR WALLETS?
I... SEE... YES. WELL.
<THEY HAVE LICENSES, YOU SEE?>
DRIVING LICENSE
<THESE PICTURES ARE BETTER, I THINK.>
<YES, THESE ARE BETTER...>
<... PLEASE ENJOY YOUR STAY IN THE ISLAMIC EMIRATE OF AFGHANISTAN.>
DRIVING LICENSE
1 HOLLAND
2 THOMAS MICHAEL
3 07/19/62
4a 12/12/02 4641/01
C2 F D2 BC B1B2

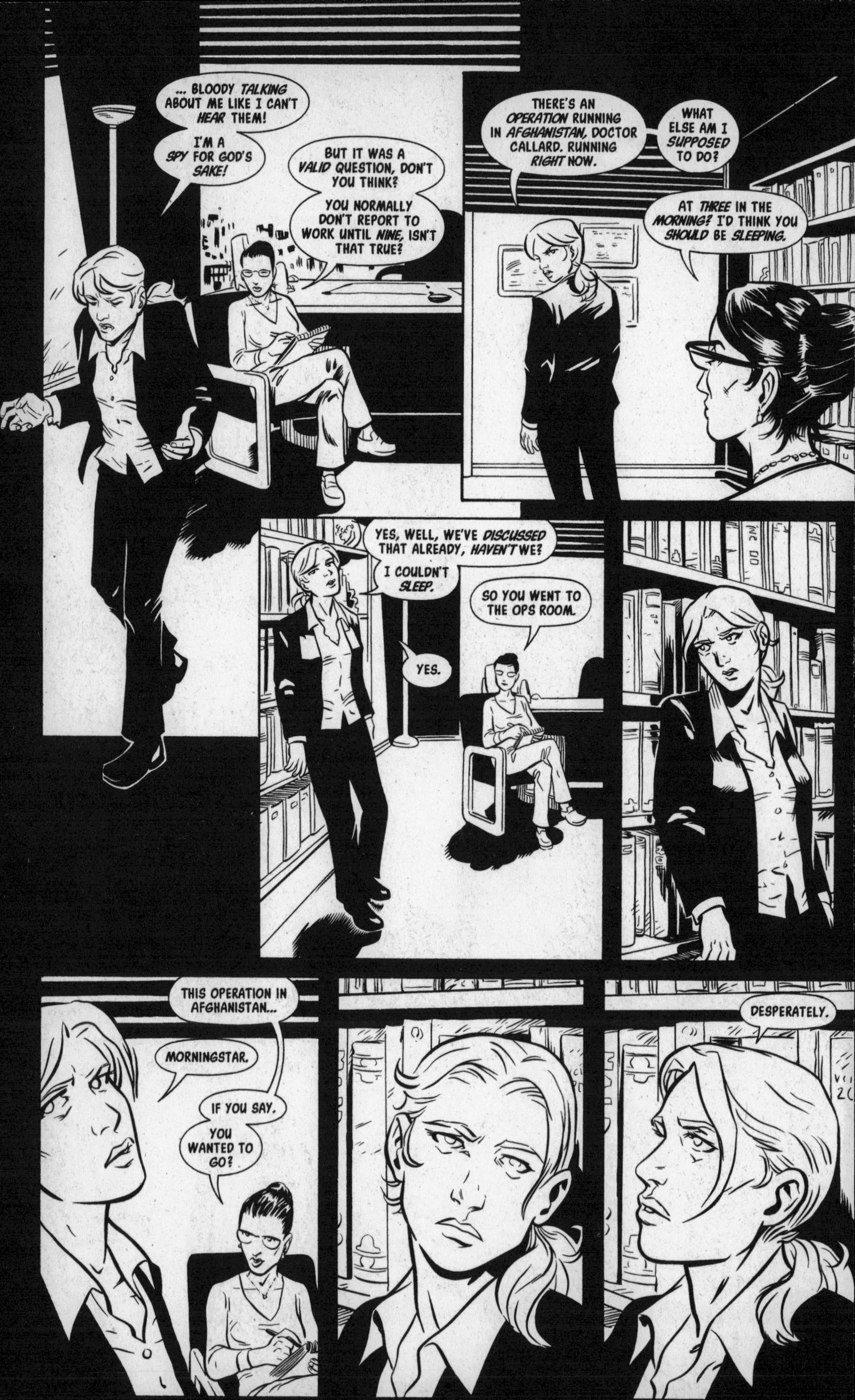
... BLOODY TALKING ABOUT ME LIKE I CAN'T HEAR THEM!
I'M A SPY FOR GOD'S SAKE!
BUT IT WAS A VALID QUESTION, DON'T YOU THINK?
YOU NORMALLY DON'T REPORT TO WORK UNTIL NINE, ISN'T THAT TRUE?
THERE'S AN OPERATION RUNNING IN AFGHANISTAN, DOCTOR CALLARD. RUNNING RIGHT NOW.
WHAT ELSE AM I SUPPOSED TO DO?
AT THREE IN THE MORNING? I'D THINK YOU SHOULD BE SLEEPING.
YES, WELL, WE'VE DISCUSSED THAT ALREADY, HAVEN'T WE?
I COULDN'T SLEEP.
SO YOU WENT TO THE OPS ROOM.
YES.
THIS OPERATION IN AFGHANISTAN...
MORNINGSTAR.
IF YOU SAY.
YOU WANTED TO GO?
DESPERATELY.

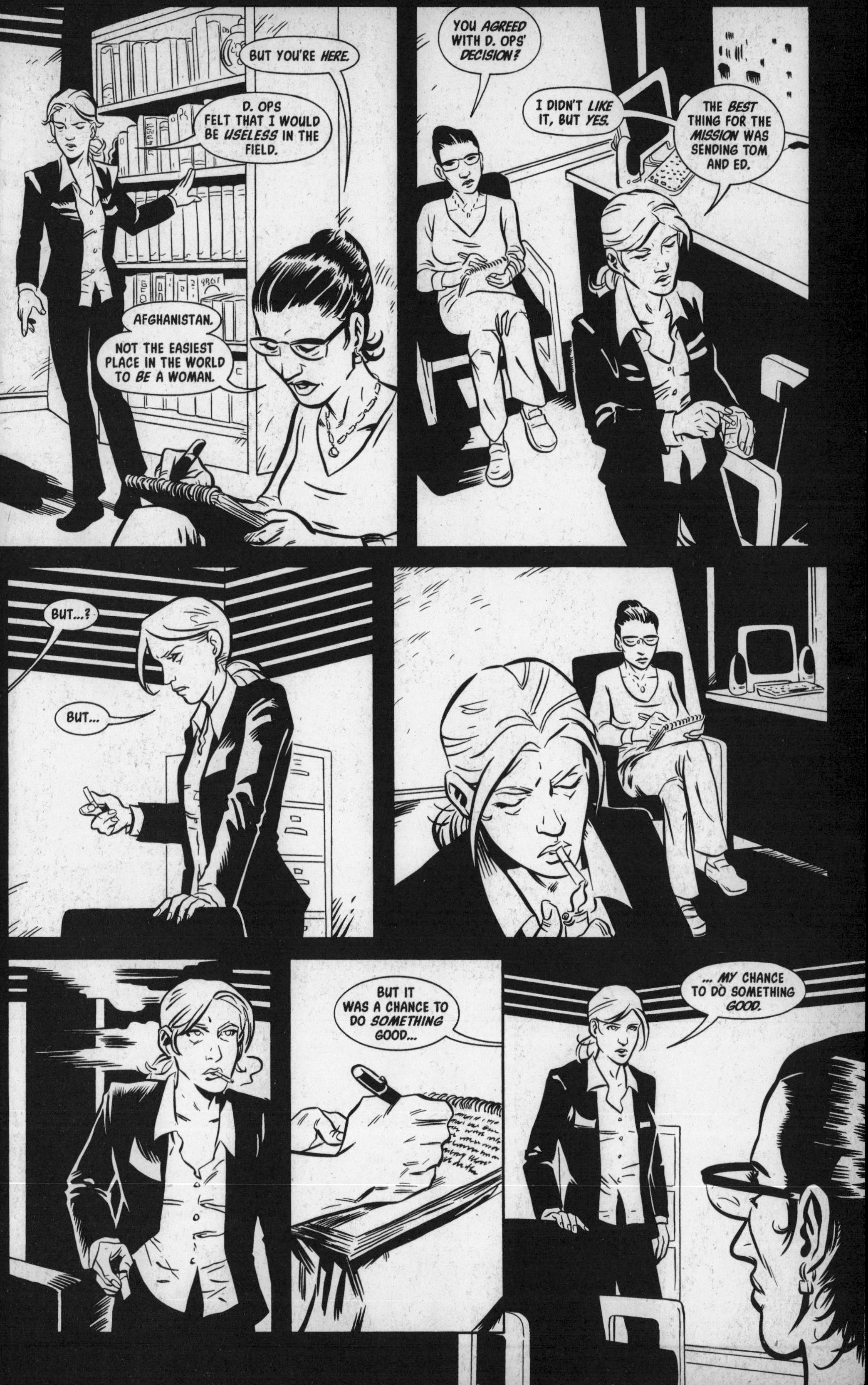

BUT YOU'RE *HERE.*
D. OPS FELT THAT I WOULD BE *USELESS* IN THE FIELD.
AFGHANISTAN.
NOT THE EASIEST PLACE IN THE WORLD TO *BE* A WOMAN.
YOU *AGREED* WITH D. OPS' *DECISION?*
I DIDN'T *LIKE* IT, BUT *YES.*
THE *BEST* THING FOR THE *MISSION* WAS SENDING TOM AND ED.
BUT...?
BUT...
BUT IT WAS A CHANCE TO DO *SOMETHING* GOOD...
... *MY* CHANCE TO DO SOMETHING *GOOD.*

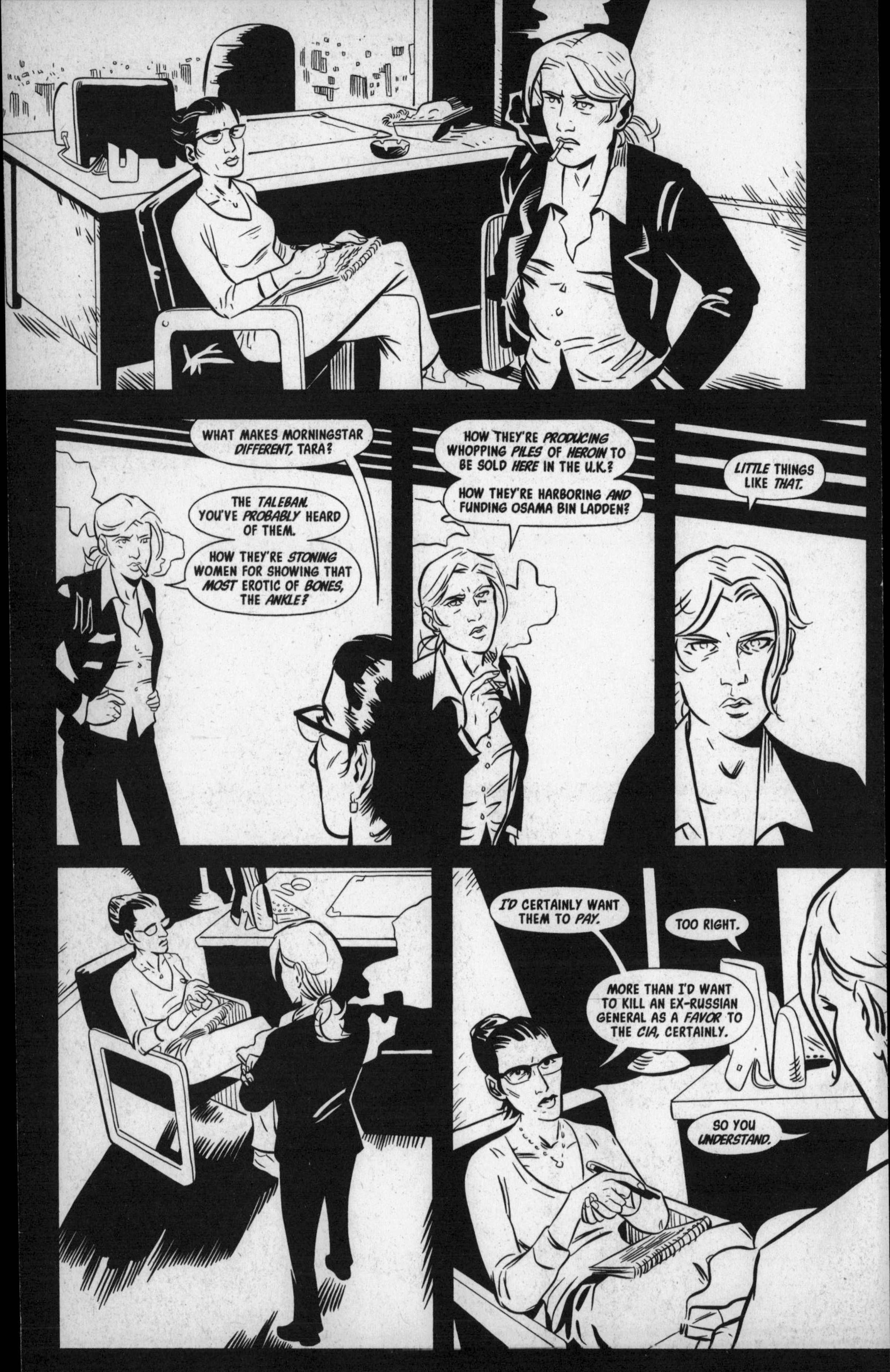
WHAT MAKES MORNINGSTAR *DIFFERENT,* TARA?
THE *TALEBAN.* YOU'VE *PROBABLY* HEARD OF THEM.
HOW THEY'RE *STONING* WOMEN FOR SHOWING THAT *MOST* EROTIC OF *BONES,* THE *ANKLE?*
HOW THEY'RE *PRODUCING* WHOPPING *PILES* OF *HEROIN* TO BE SOLD *HERE* IN THE U.K.?
HOW THEY'RE HARBORING *AND* FUNDING OSAMA BIN LADDEN?
LITTLE THINGS LIKE *THAT.*
I'D CERTAINLY WANT THEM TO *PAY.*
TOO RIGHT.
MORE THAN I'D WANT TO KILL AN EX-RUSSIAN GENERAL AS A *FAVOR* TO THE *CIA,* CERTAINLY.
SO YOU *UNDERSTAND.*

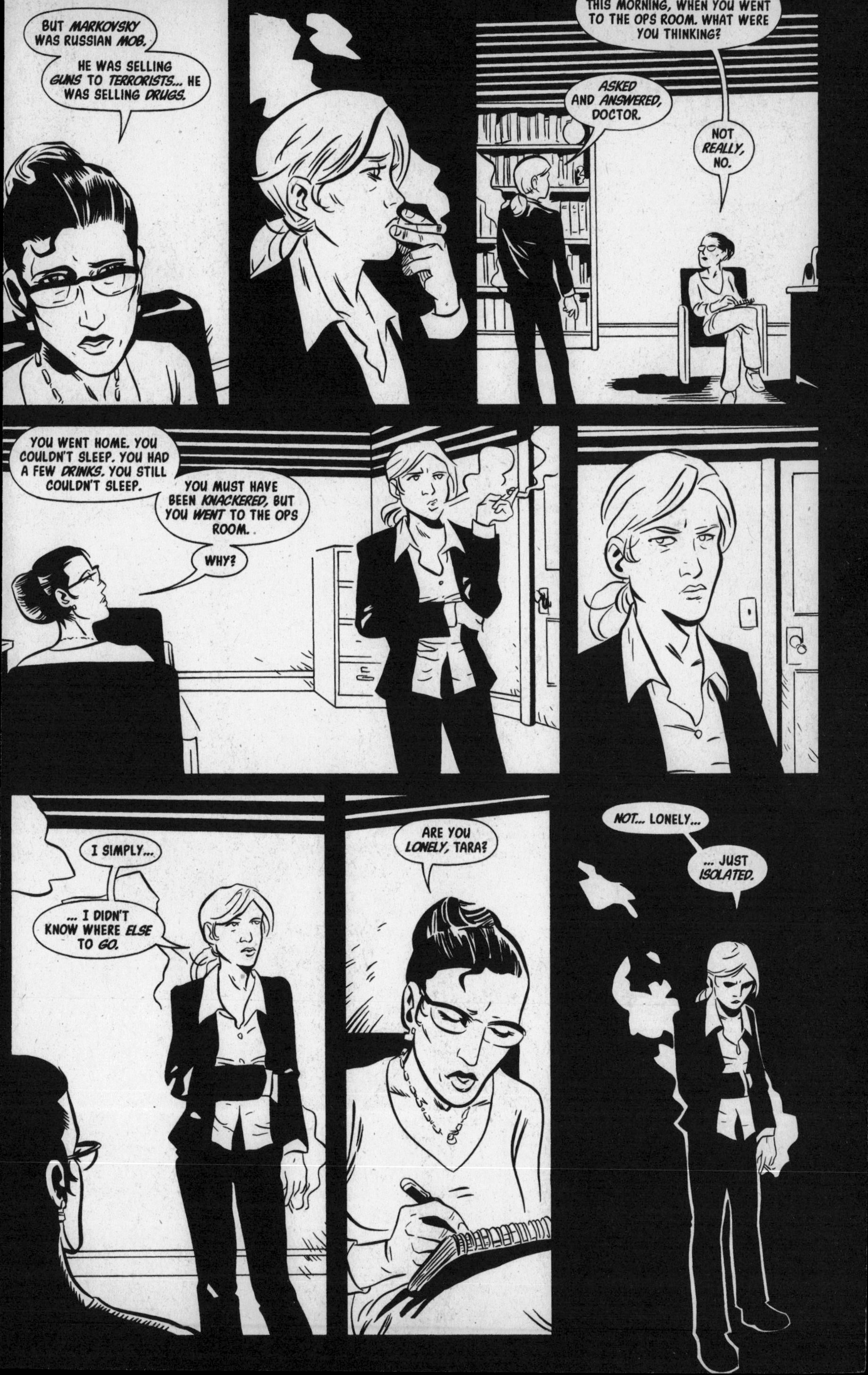
BUT MARKOVSKY WAS RUSSIAN MOB.
HE WAS SELLING GUNS TO TERRORISTS... HE WAS SELLING DRUGS.
THIS MORNING, WHEN YOU WENT TO THE OPS ROOM. WHAT WERE YOU THINKING?
ASKED AND ANSWERED, DOCTOR.
NOT REALLY, NO.
YOU WENT HOME. YOU COULDN'T SLEEP. YOU HAD A FEW DRINKS. YOU STILL COULDN'T SLEEP.
YOU MUST HAVE BEEN KNACKERED, BUT YOU WENT TO THE OPS ROOM.
WHY?
I SIMPLY...
... I DIDN'T KNOW WHERE ELSE TO GO.
ARE YOU LONELY, TARA?
NOT... LONELY...
... JUST ISOLATED.

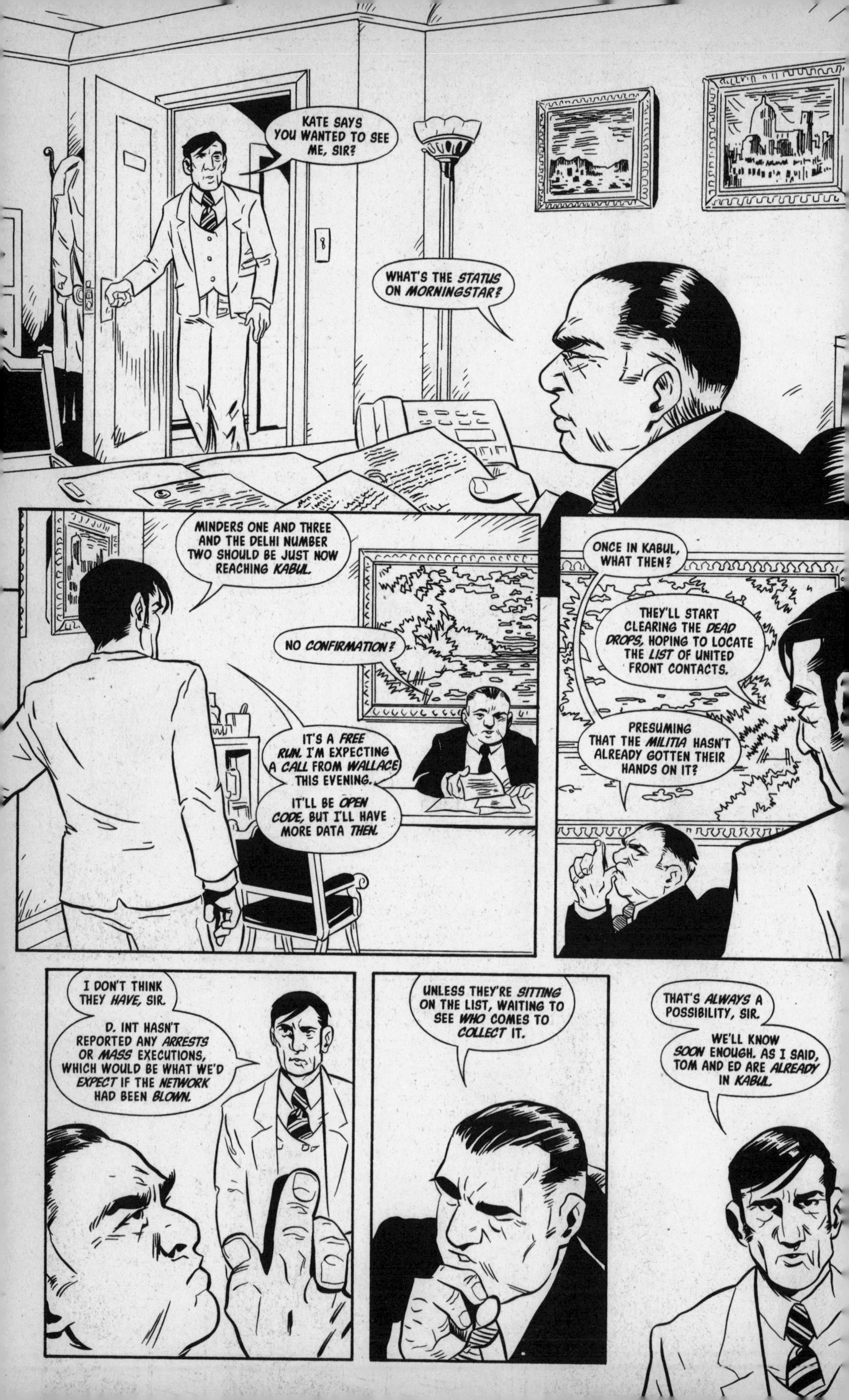
KATE SAYS YOU WANTED TO SEE ME, SIR?
WHAT'S THE STATUS ON MORNINGSTAR?
MINDERS ONE AND THREE AND THE DELHI NUMBER TWO SHOULD BE JUST NOW REACHING KABUL.
NO CONFIRMATION?
IT'S A FREE RUN. I'M EXPECTING A CALL FROM WALLACE THIS EVENING.
IT'LL BE OPEN CODE, BUT I'LL HAVE MORE DATA THEN.
ONCE IN KABUL, WHAT THEN?
THEY'LL START CLEARING THE DEAD DROPS, HOPING TO LOCATE THE LIST OF UNITED FRONT CONTACTS.
PRESUMING THAT THE MILITIA HASN'T ALREADY GOTTEN THEIR HANDS ON IT?
I DON'T THINK THEY HAVE, SIR.
D. INT HASN'T REPORTED ANY ARRESTS OR MASS EXECUTIONS, WHICH WOULD BE WHAT WE'D EXPECT IF THE NETWORK HAD BEEN BLOWN.
UNLESS THEY'RE SITTING ON THE LIST, WAITING TO SEE WHO COMES TO COLLECT IT.
THAT'S ALWAYS A POSSIBILITY, SIR.
WE'LL KNOW SOON ENOUGH. AS I SAID, TOM AND ED ARE ALREADY IN KABUL.

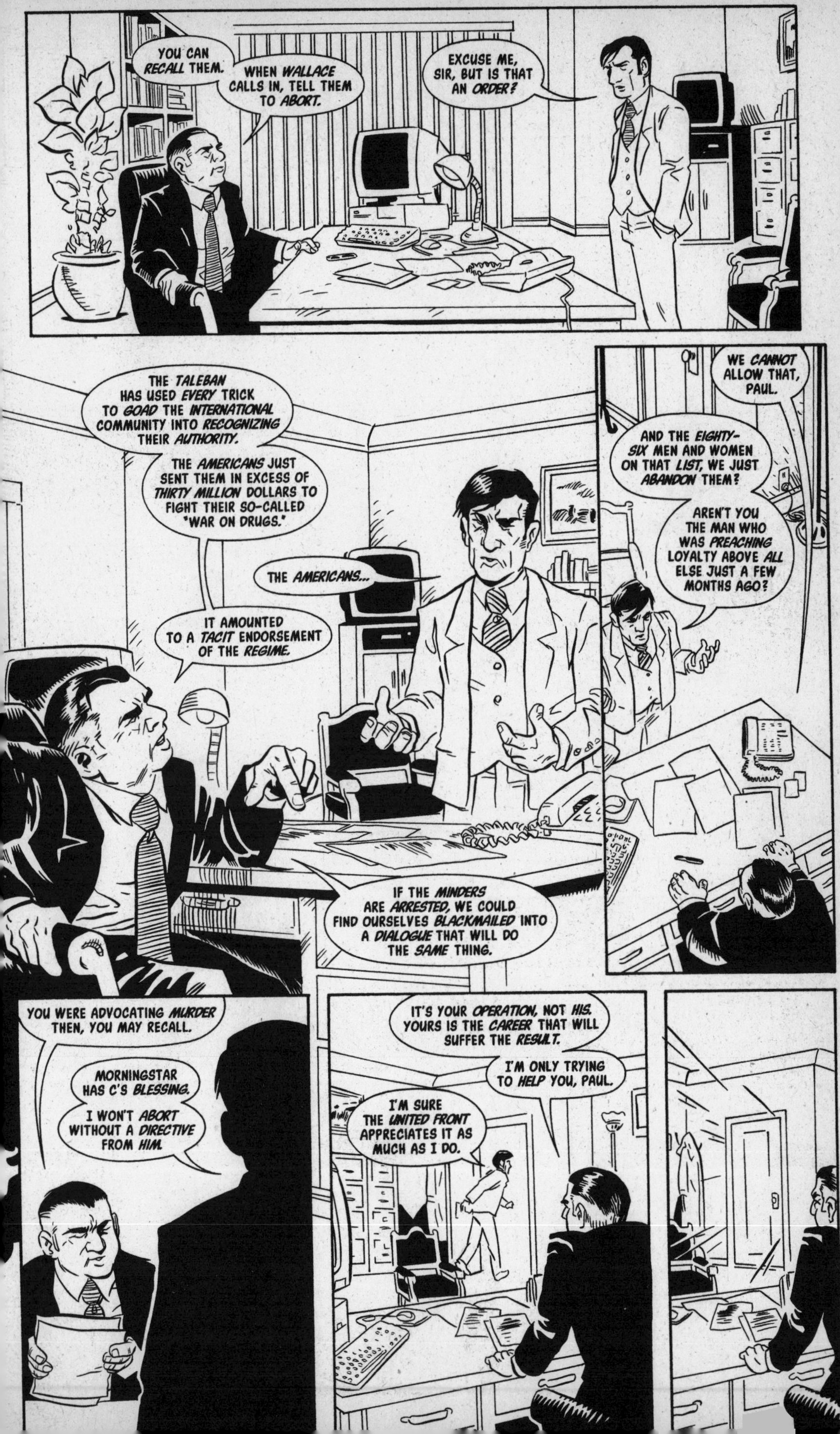
YOU CAN RECALL THEM.
WHEN WALLACE CALLS IN, TELL THEM TO ABORT.
EXCUSE ME, SIR, BUT IS THAT AN ORDER?
THE TALEBAN HAS USED EVERY TRICK TO GOAD THE INTERNATIONAL COMMUNITY INTO RECOGNIZING THEIR AUTHORITY.
THE AMERICANS JUST SENT THEM IN EXCESS OF THIRTY MILLION DOLLARS TO FIGHT THEIR SO-CALLED "WAR ON DRUGS."
THE AMERICANS...
IT AMOUNTED TO A TACIT ENDORSEMENT OF THE REGIME.
IF THE MINDERS ARE ARRESTED, WE COULD FIND OURSELVES BLACKMAILED INTO A DIALOGUE THAT WILL DO THE SAME THING.
WE CANNOT ALLOW THAT, PAUL.
AND THE EIGHTY-SIX MEN AND WOMEN ON THAT LIST, WE JUST ABANDON THEM?
AREN'T YOU THE MAN WHO WAS PREACHING LOYALTY ABOVE ALL ELSE JUST A FEW MONTHS AGO?
YOU WERE ADVOCATING MURDER THEN, YOU MAY RECALL.
MORNINGSTAR HAS C'S BLESSING.
I WON'T ABORT WITHOUT A DIRECTIVE FROM HIM.
IT'S YOUR OPERATION, NOT HIS. YOURS IS THE CAREER THAT WILL SUFFER THE RESULT.
I'M ONLY TRYING TO HELP YOU, PAUL.
I'M SURE THE UNITED FRONT APPRECIATES IT AS MUCH AS I DO.

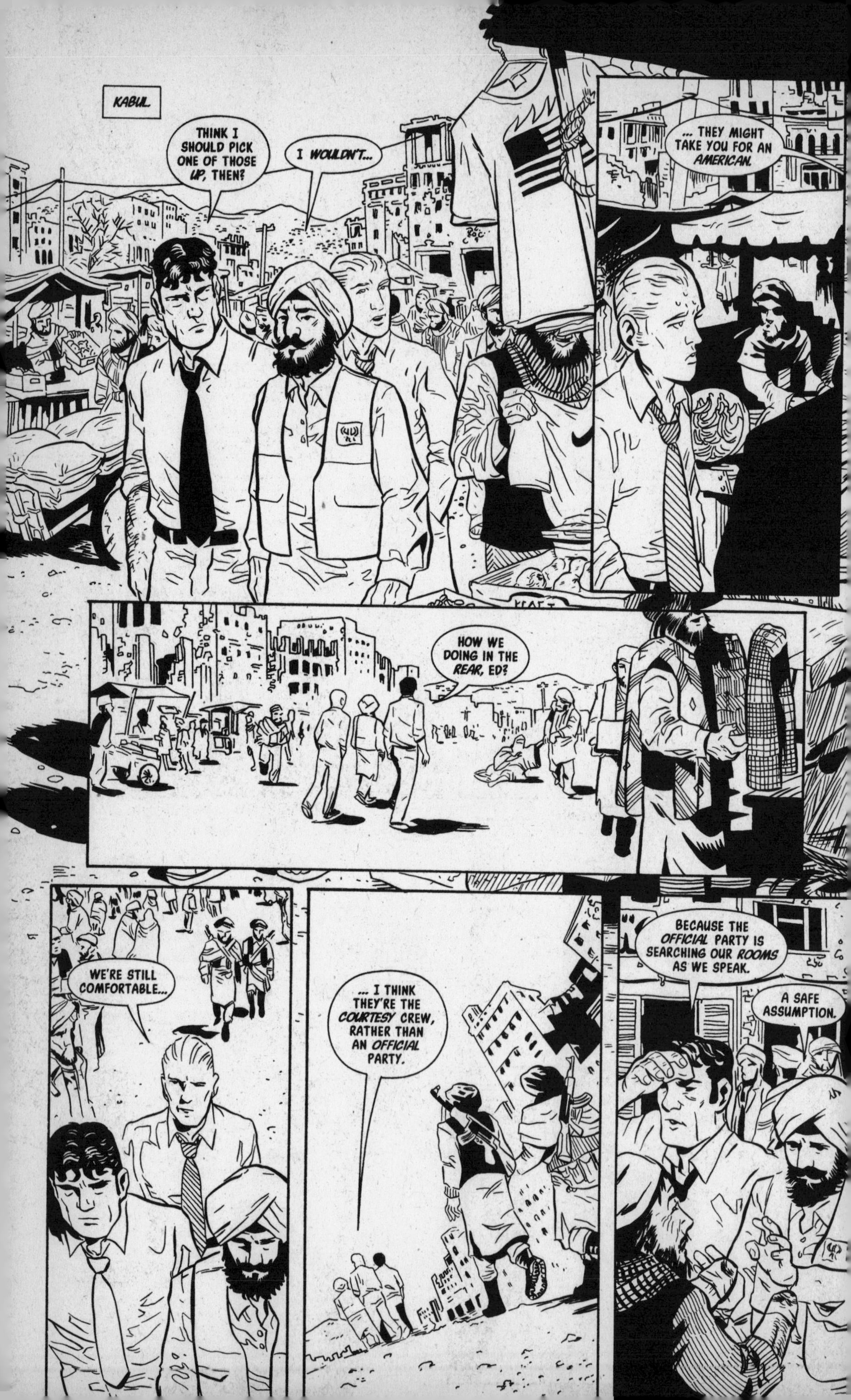
KABUL.
THINK I SHOULD PICK ONE OF THOSE UP, THEN?
I WOULDN'T...
... THEY MIGHT TAKE YOU FOR AN AMERICAN.
HOW WE DOING IN THE REAR, ED?
WE'RE STILL COMFORTABLE...
... I THINK THEY'RE THE COURTESY CREW, RATHER THAN AN OFFICIAL PARTY.
BECAUSE THE OFFICIAL PARTY IS SEARCHING OUR ROOMS AS WE SPEAK.
A SAFE ASSUMPTION.

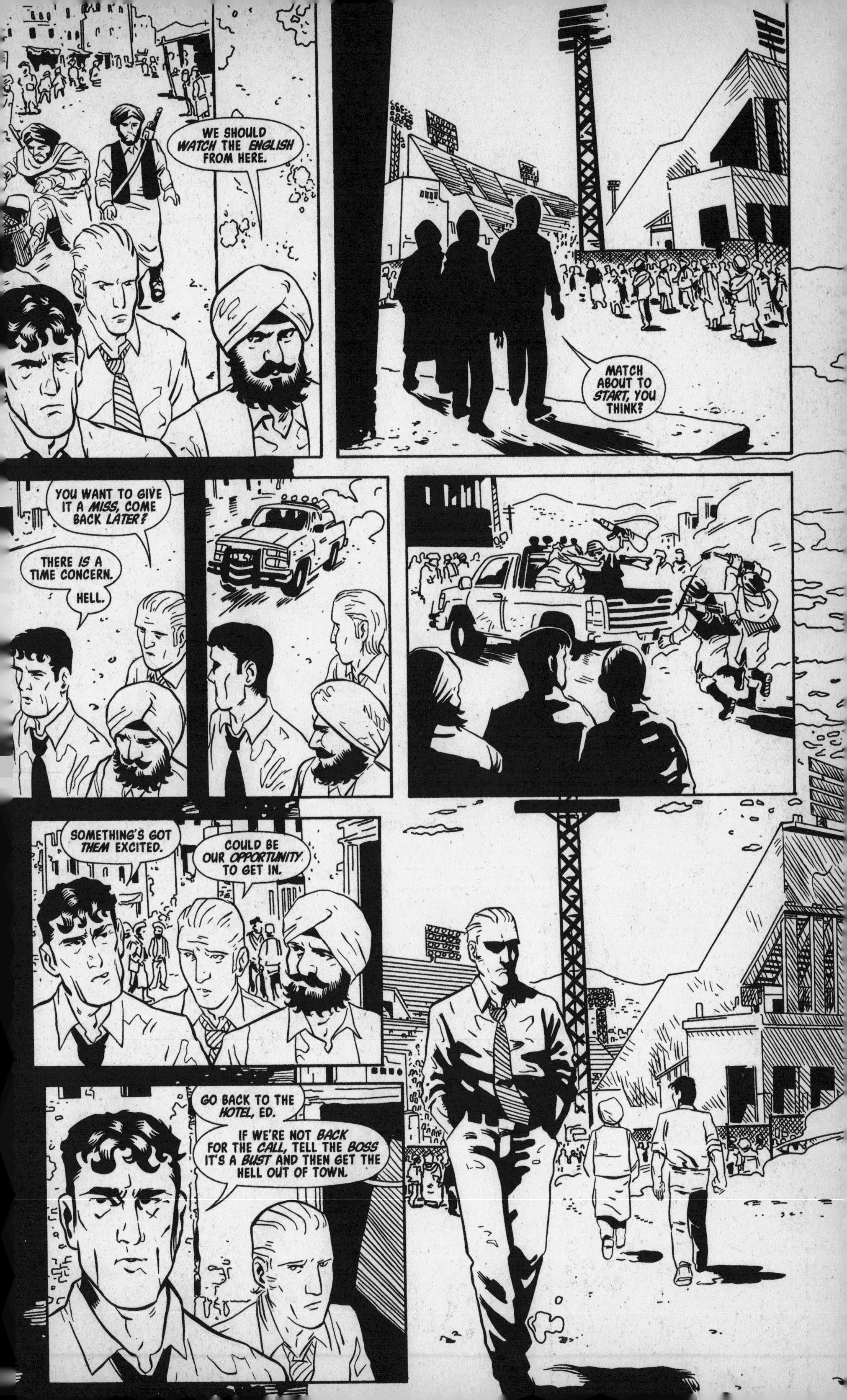
WE SHOULD WATCH THE ENGLISH FROM HERE.
MATCH ABOUT TO START, YOU THINK?
YOU WANT TO GIVE IT A MISS, COME BACK LATER?
THERE IS A TIME CONCERN.
HELL.
SOMETHING'S GOT THEM EXCITED.
COULD BE OUR OPPORTUNITY TO GET IN.
GO BACK TO THE HOTEL, ED.
IF WE'RE NOT BACK FOR THE CALL, TELL THE BOSS IT'S A BUST AND THEN GET THE HELL OUT OF TOWN.

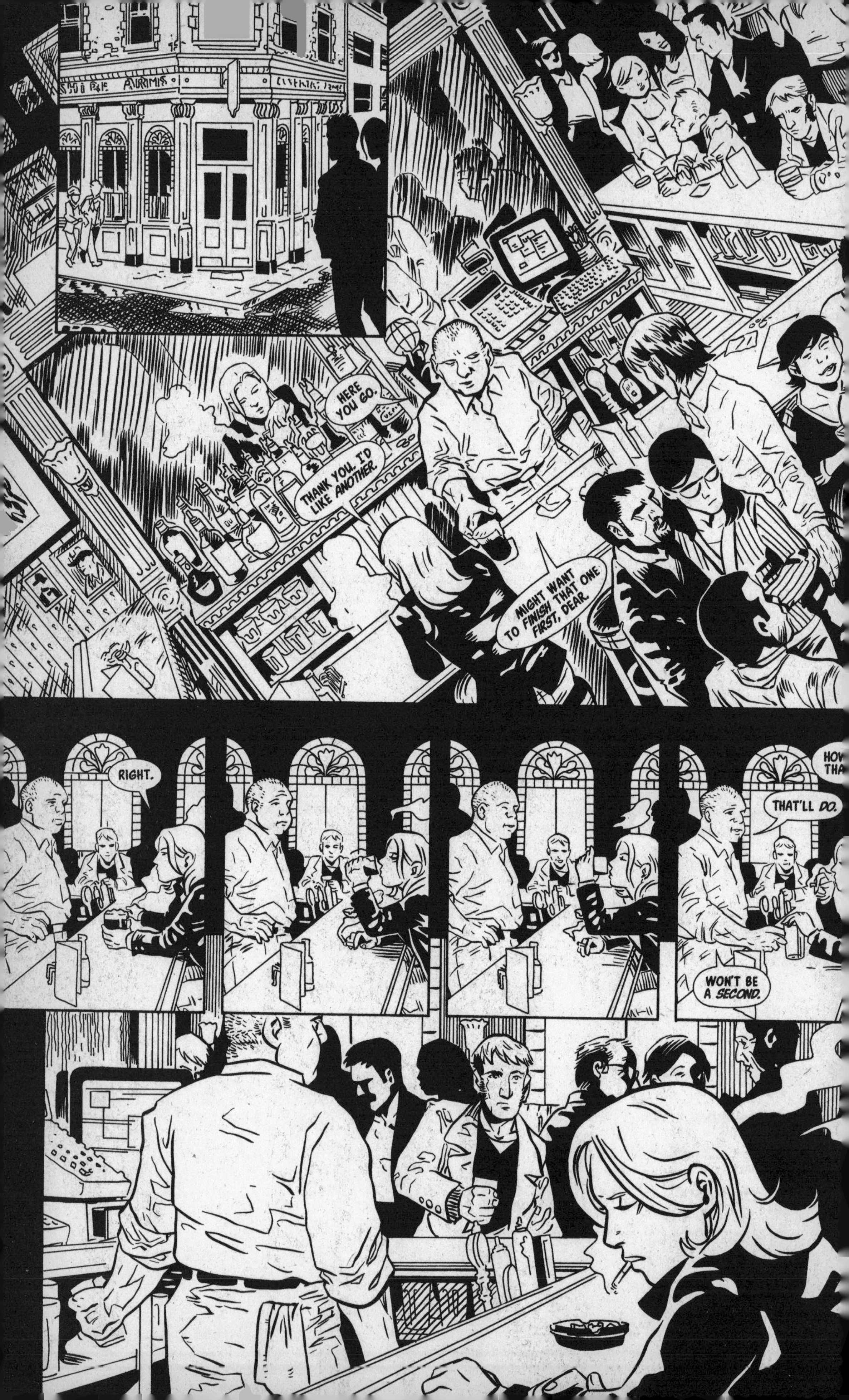
HERE YOU GO.
THANK YOU. I'D LIKE ANOTHER.
MIGHT WANT TO FINISH THAT ONE FIRST, DEAR.
RIGHT.
THAT'LL DO.
WON'T BE A SECOND.

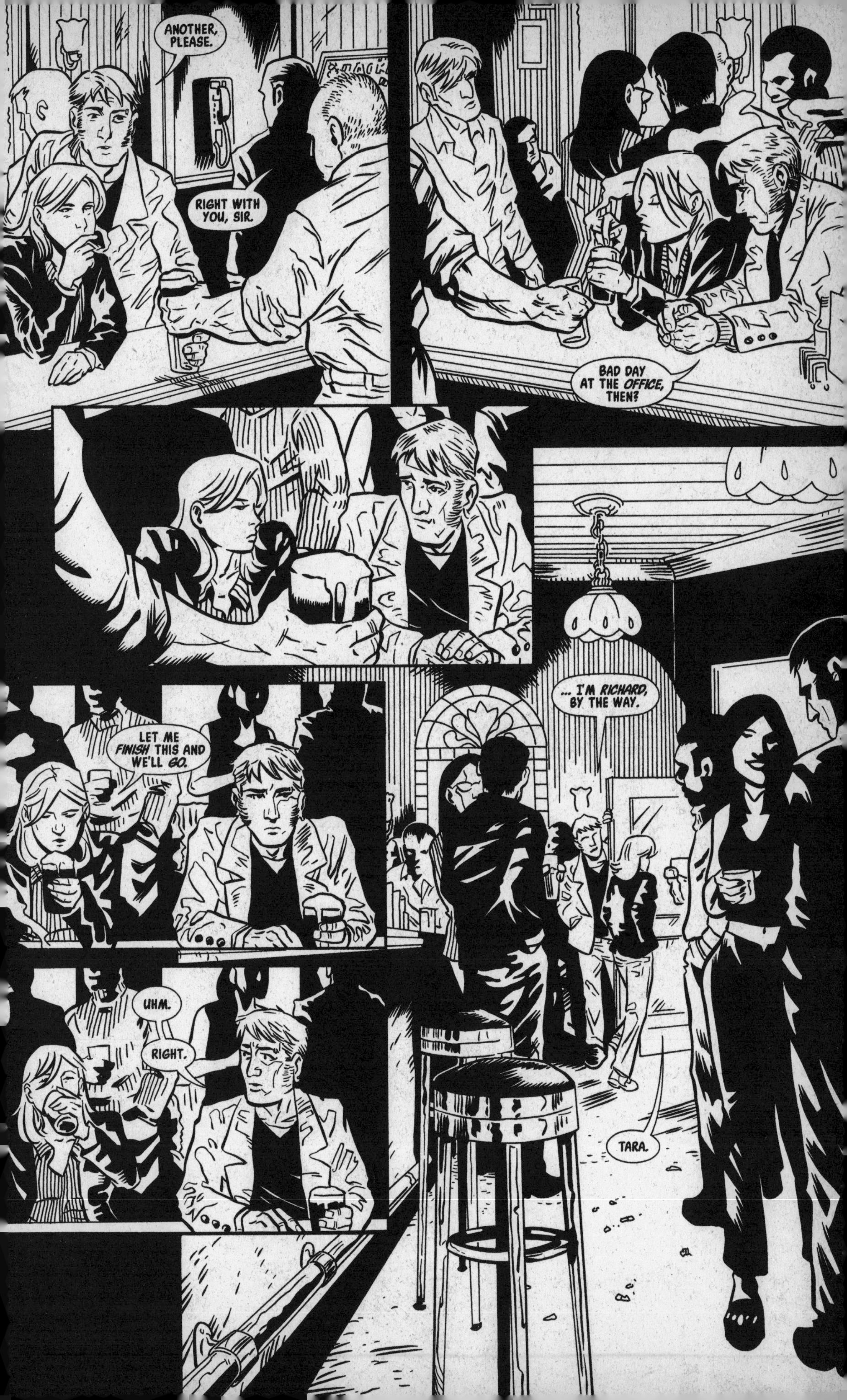
ANOTHER, PLEASE.
RIGHT WITH YOU, SIR.
BAD DAY AT THE *OFFICE*, THEN?
LET ME *FINISH* THIS AND WE'LL *GO*.
UHM.
RIGHT.
... I'M *RICHARD*, BY THE WAY.
TARA.

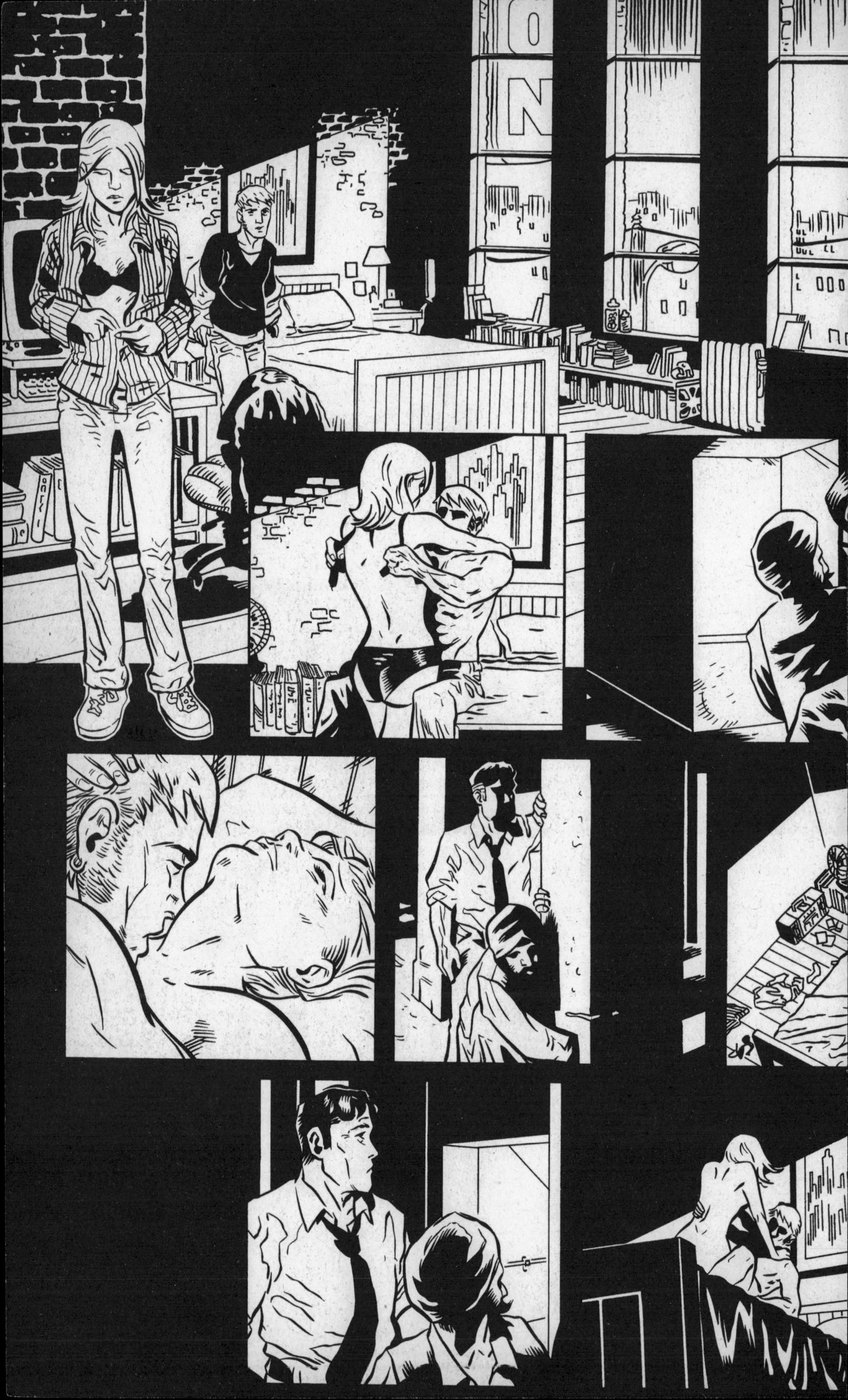

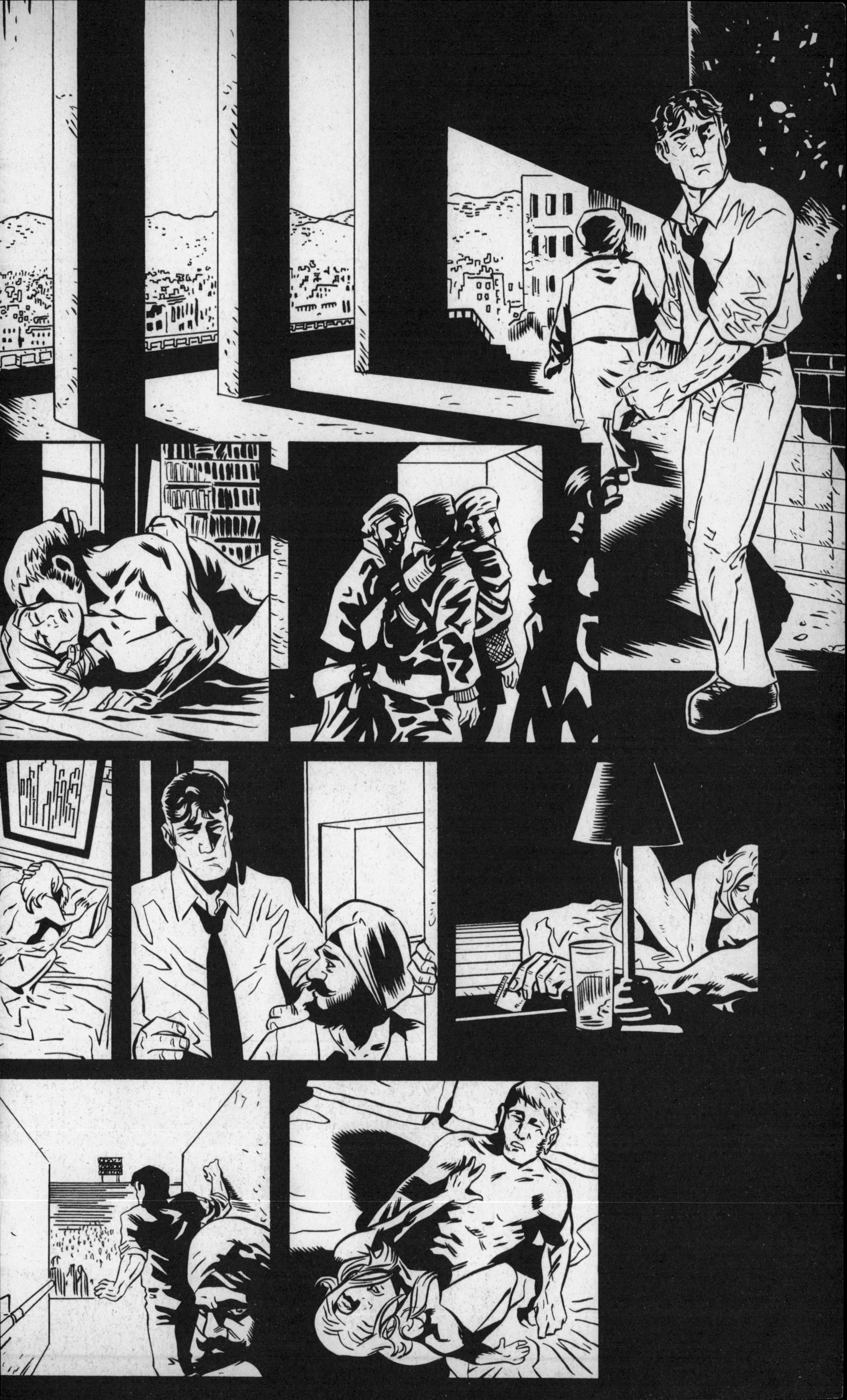

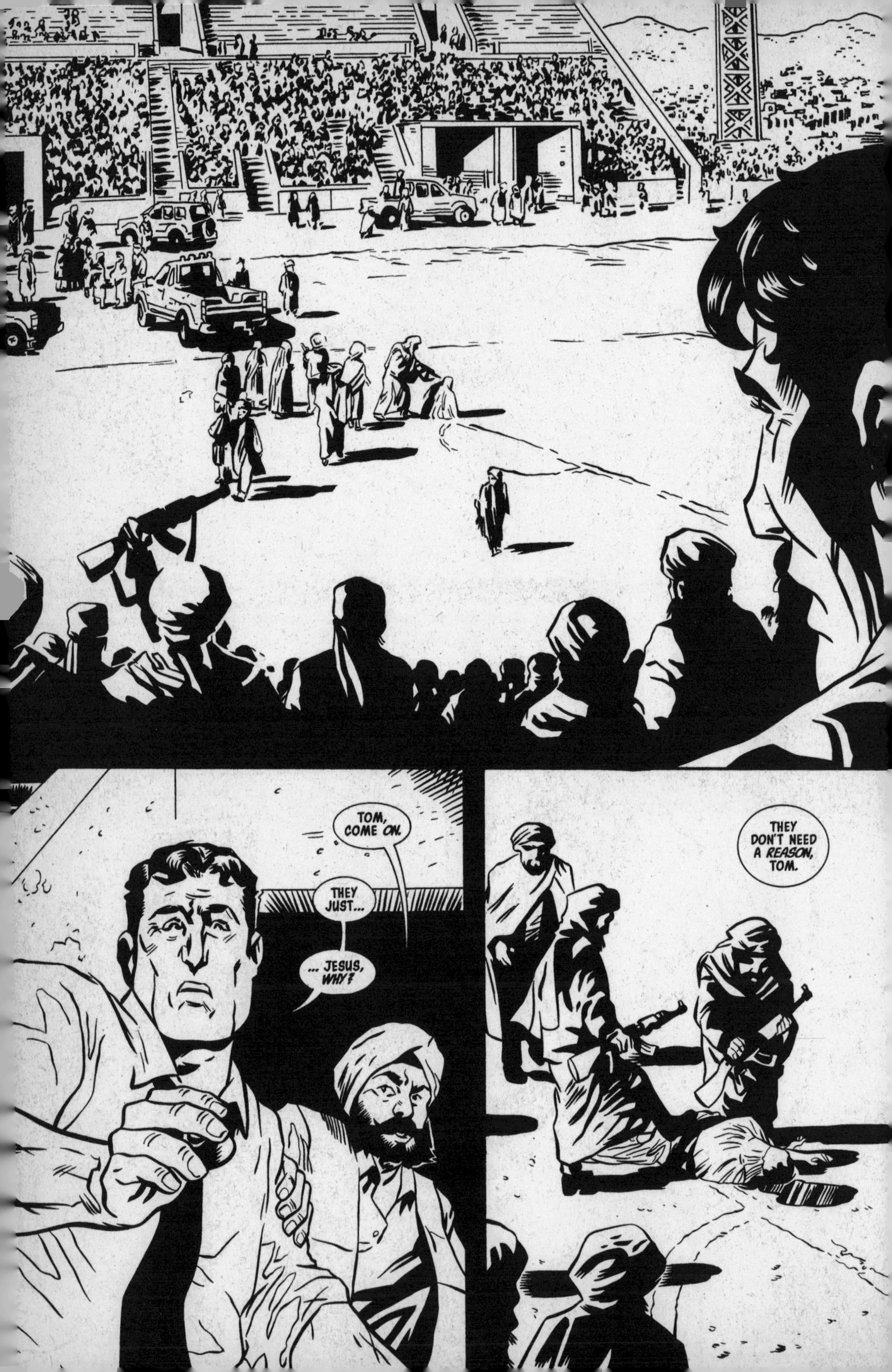
TOM, COME ON.
THEY JUST...
... JESUS, WHY?
THEY DON'T NEED A REASON, TOM.

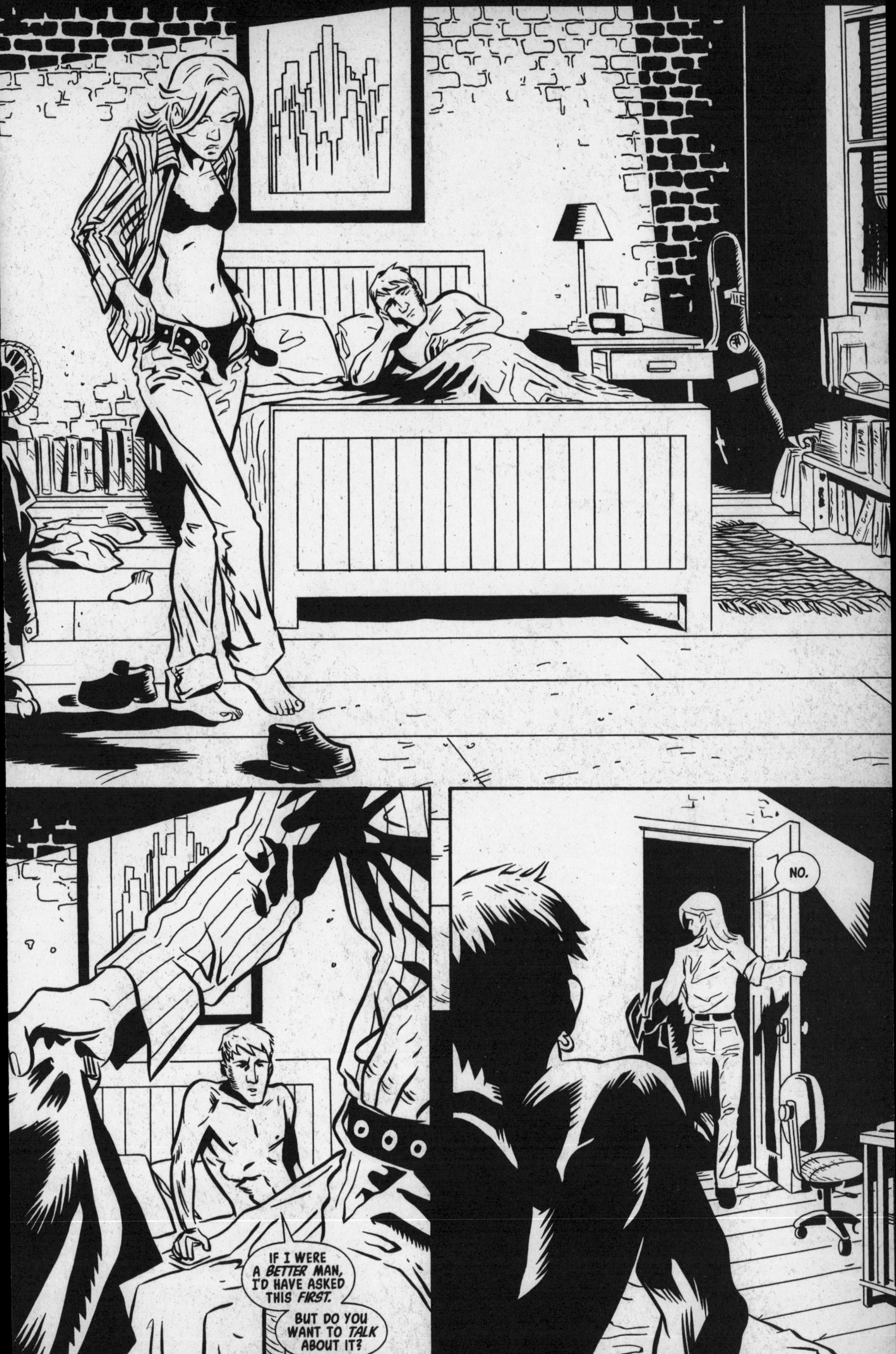
IF I WERE A *BETTER* MAN, I'D HAVE ASKED THIS *FIRST*.
BUT DO YOU WANT TO *TALK* ABOUT IT?
NO.

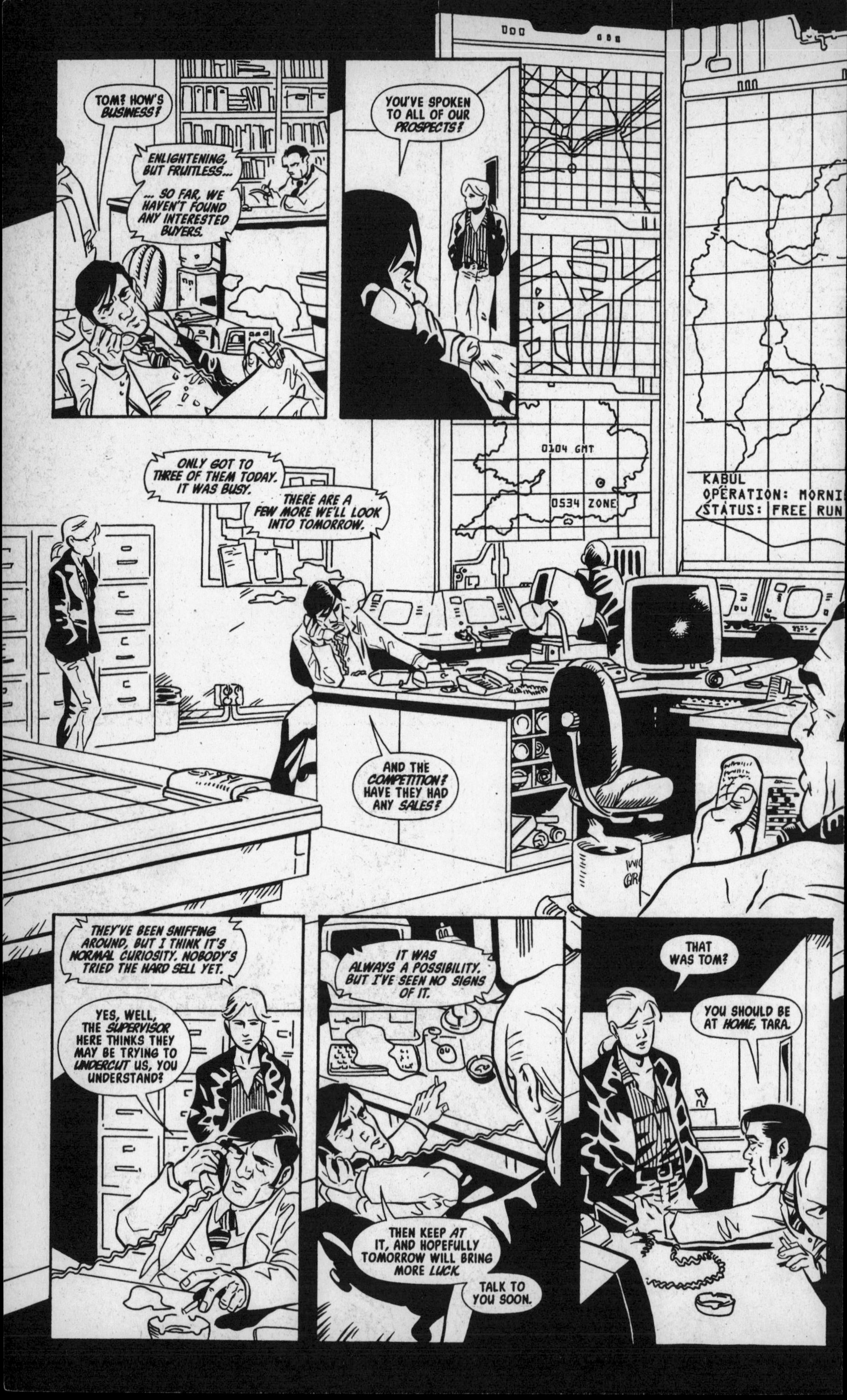

TOM? HOW'S BUSINESS?
ENLIGHTENING, BUT FRUITLESS...
... SO FAR, WE HAVEN'T FOUND ANY INTERESTED BUYERS.
YOU'VE SPOKEN TO ALL OF OUR PROSPECTS?
ONLY GOT TO THREE OF THEM TODAY. IT WAS BUSY.
THERE ARE A FEW MORE WE'LL LOOK INTO TOMORROW.
0104 GMT
0534 ZONE
KABUL
OPERATION: MORNI
STATUS: FREE RUN
AND THE COMPETITION? HAVE THEY HAD ANY SALES?
THEY'VE BEEN SNIFFING AROUND, BUT I THINK IT'S NORMAL CURIOSITY. NOBODY'S TRIED THE HARD SELL YET.
YES, WELL, THE SUPERVISOR HERE THINKS THEY MAY BE TRYING TO UNDERCUT US, YOU UNDERSTAND?
IT WAS ALWAYS A POSSIBILITY. BUT I'VE SEEN NO SIGNS OF IT.
THEN KEEP AT IT, AND HOPEFULLY TOMORROW WILL BRING MORE LUCK.
TALK TO YOU SOON.
THAT WAS TOM?
YOU SHOULD BE AT HOME, TARA.

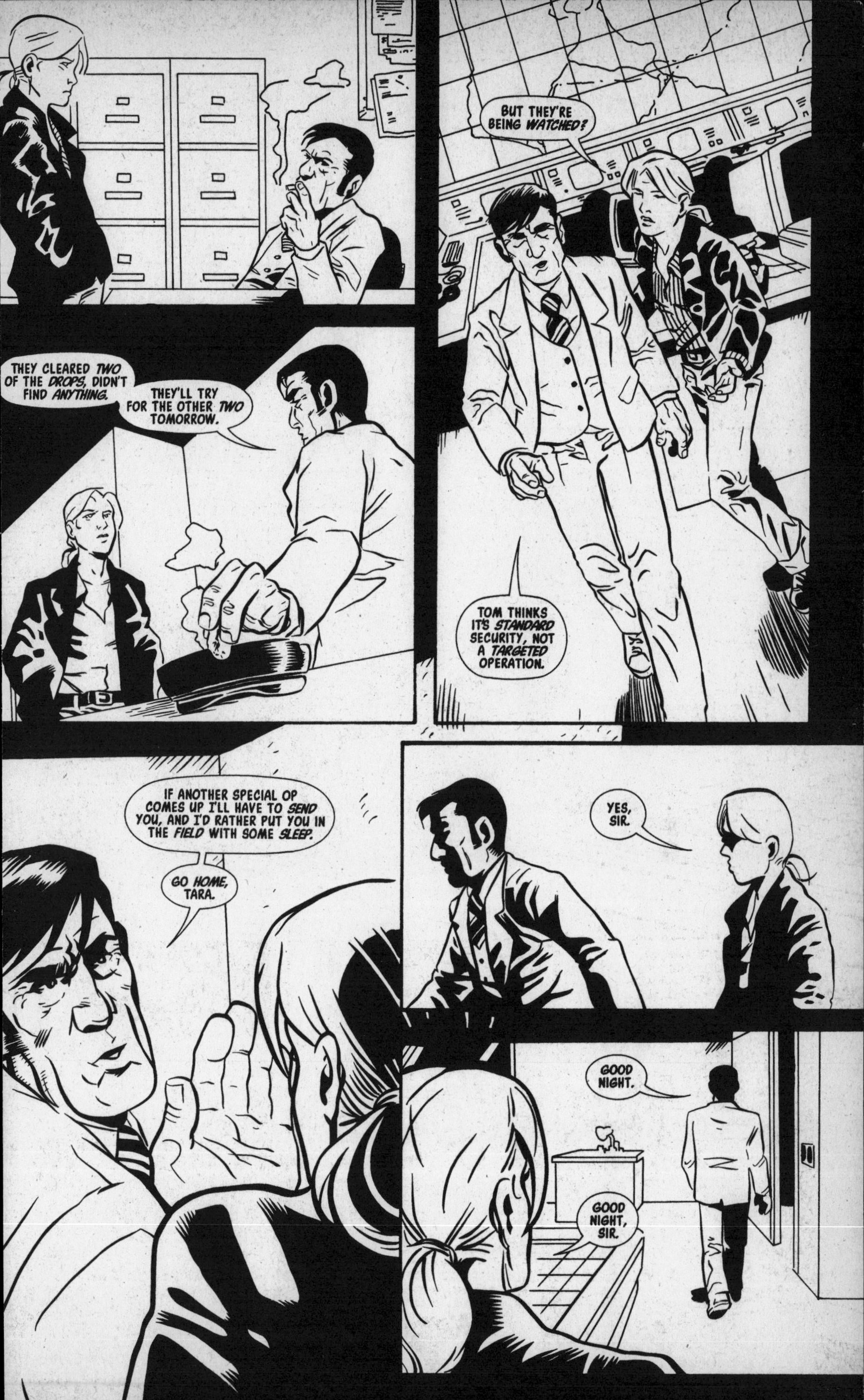
BUT THEY'RE BEING *WATCHED*?
THEY CLEARED *TWO* OF THE *DROPS*, DIDN'T FIND *ANYTHING*.
THEY'LL TRY FOR THE OTHER *TWO* TOMORROW.
TOM THINKS IT'S *STANDARD* SECURITY, NOT A *TARGETED* OPERATION.
IF ANOTHER SPECIAL OP COMES UP I'LL HAVE TO *SEND* YOU, AND I'D RATHER PUT YOU IN THE *FIELD* WITH SOME *SLEEP*.
GO *HOME*, TARA.
YES, SIR.
GOOD NIGHT.
GOOD NIGHT, SIR.

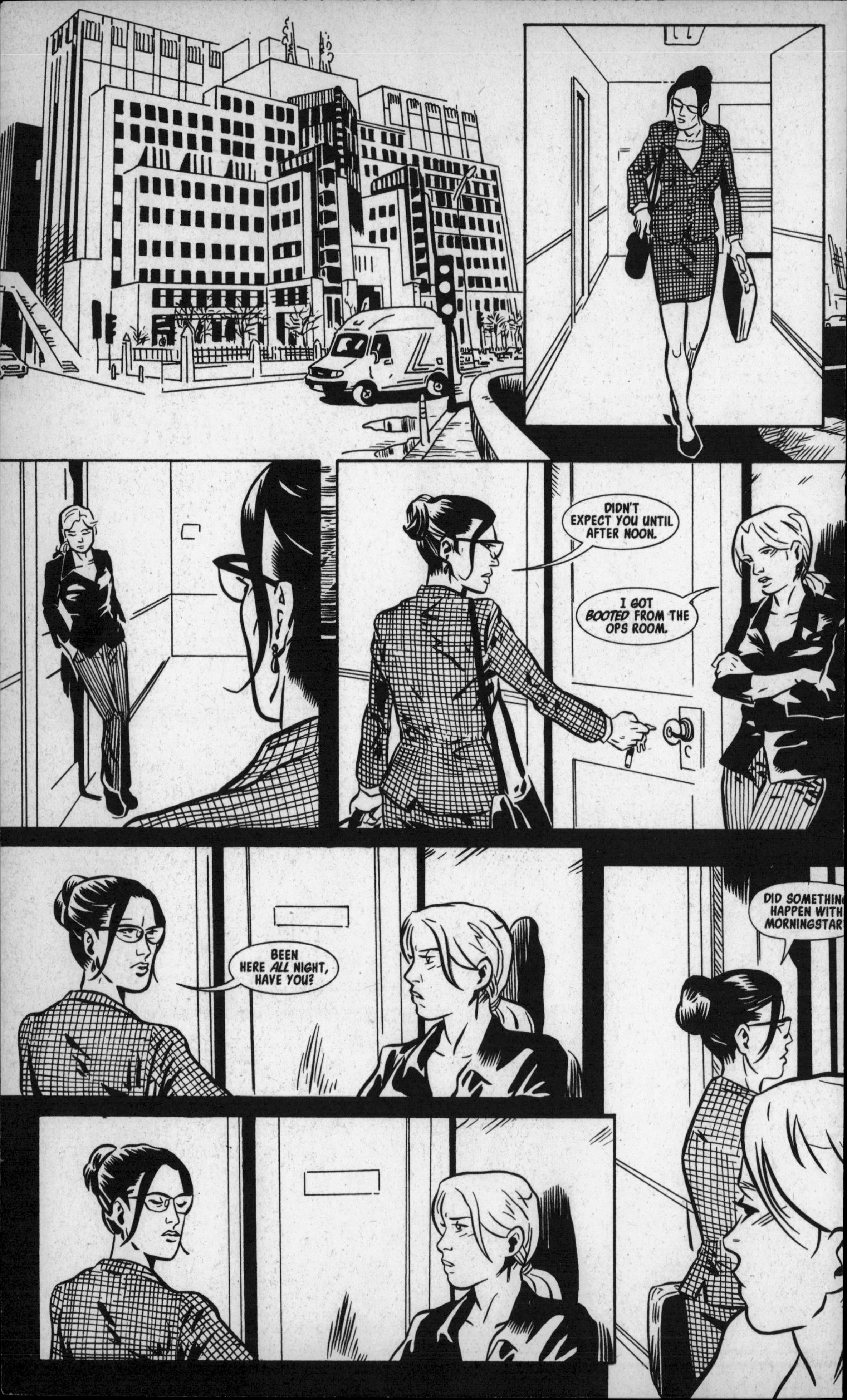
DIDN'T EXPECT YOU UNTIL AFTER NOON.
I GOT *BOOTED* FROM THE OPS ROOM.
BEEN HERE *ALL* NIGHT, HAVE YOU?
DID SOMETHING HAPPEN WITH MORNINGSTAR

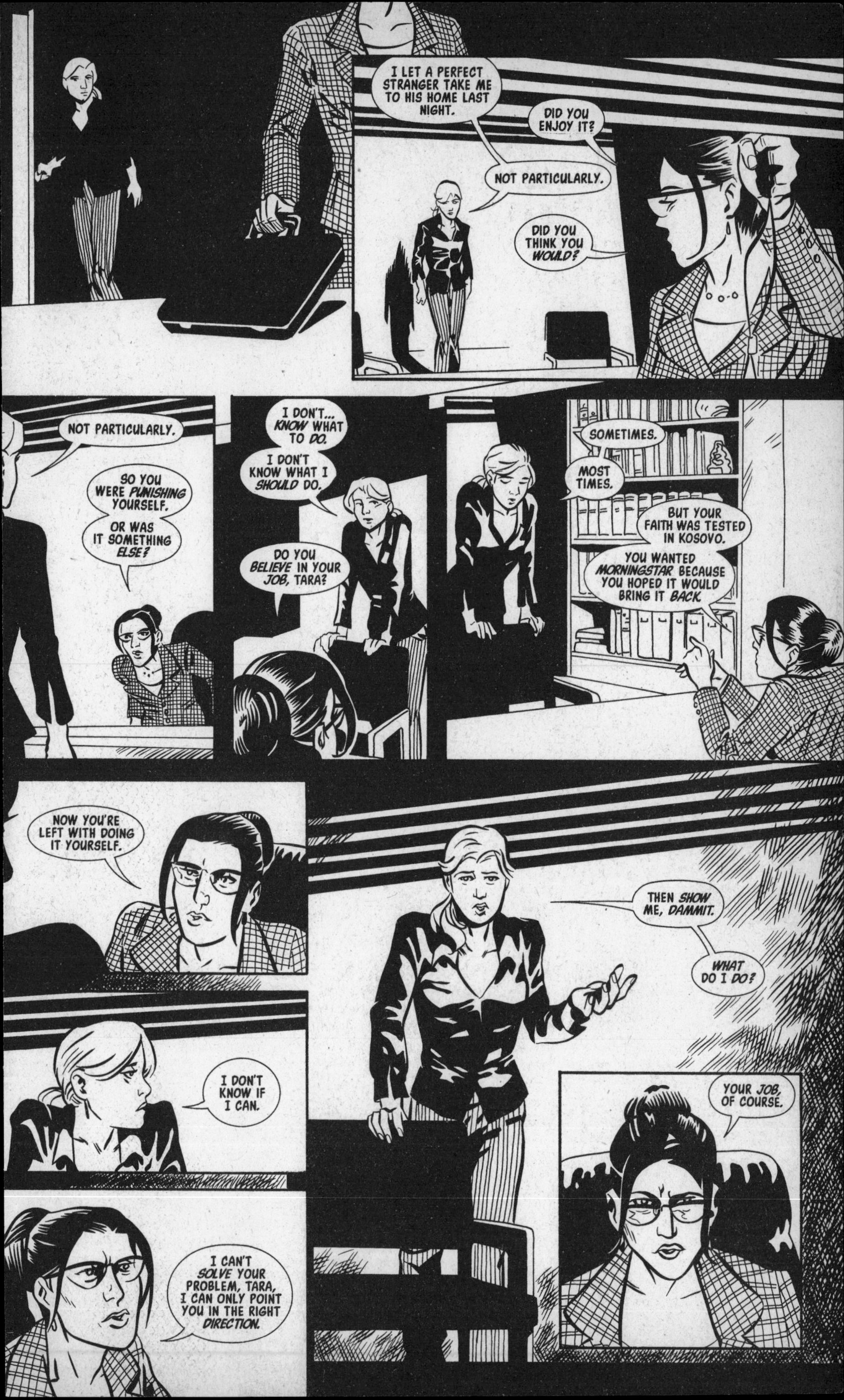
I LET A PERFECT STRANGER TAKE ME TO HIS HOME LAST NIGHT.
DID YOU ENJOY IT?
NOT PARTICULARLY.
DID YOU THINK YOU *WOULD?*
NOT PARTICULARLY.
SO YOU WERE *PUNISHING* YOURSELF.
OR WAS IT SOMETHING *ELSE?*
I DON'T... *KNOW* WHAT TO *DO.*
I DON'T KNOW WHAT I *SHOULD* DO.
DO YOU *BELIEVE* IN YOUR *JOB,* TARA?
SOMETIMES.
MOST TIMES.
BUT YOUR FAITH WAS TESTED IN KOSOVO.
YOU WANTED *MORNINGSTAR* BECAUSE YOU HOPED IT WOULD BRING IT *BACK.*
NOW YOU'RE LEFT WITH DOING IT YOURSELF.
THEN *SHOW* ME, *DAMMIT.*
WHAT DO I *DO?*
I DON'T KNOW IF I CAN.
YOUR *JOB,* OF COURSE.
I CAN'T *SOLVE* YOUR PROBLEM, TARA, I CAN ONLY POINT YOU IN THE RIGHT *DIRECTION.*

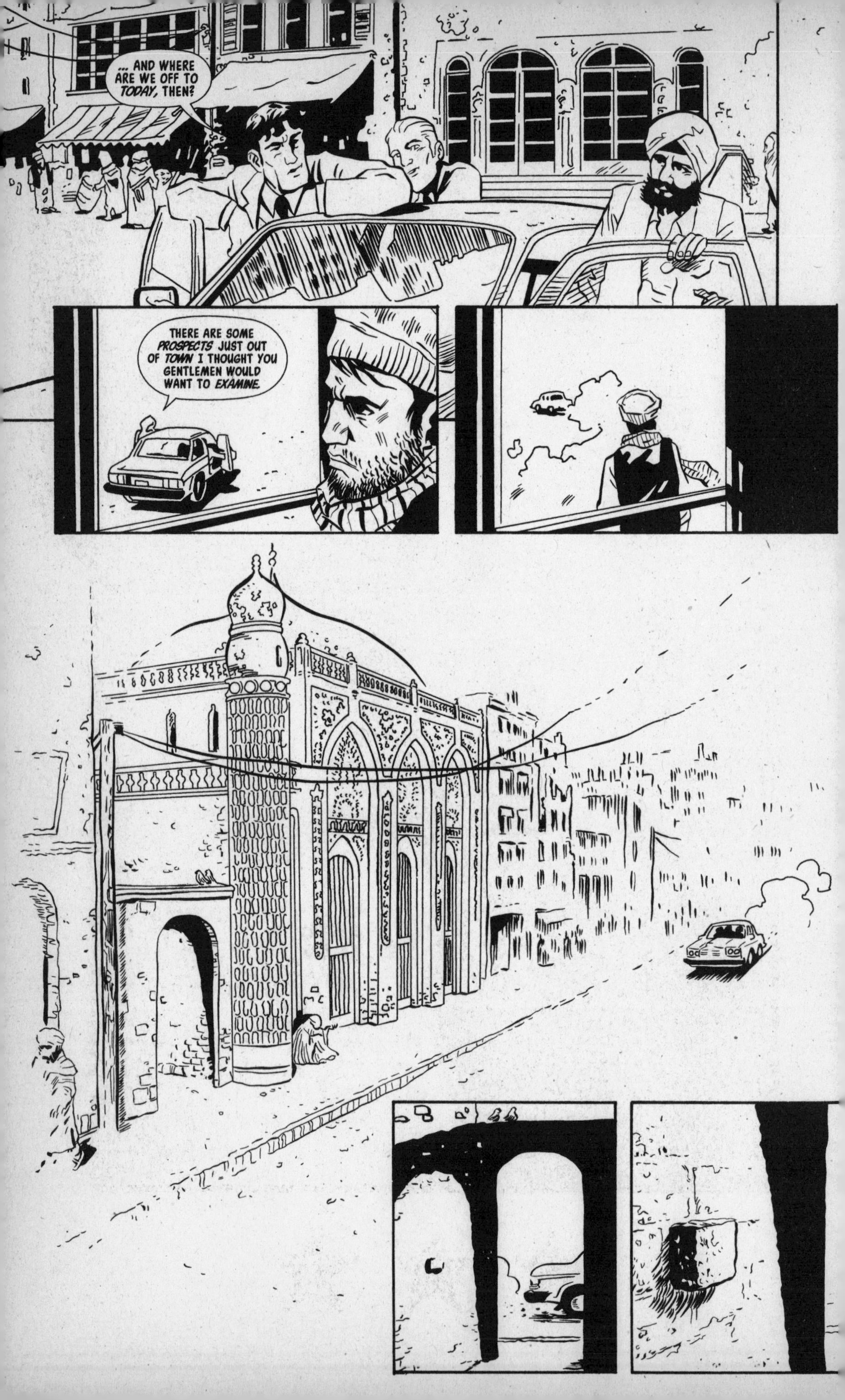
... AND WHERE ARE WE OFF TO *TODAY*, THEN?
THERE ARE SOME *PROSPECTS* JUST OUT OF *TOWN* I THOUGHT YOU GENTLEMEN WOULD WANT TO *EXAMINE*.

CHAPTER 3

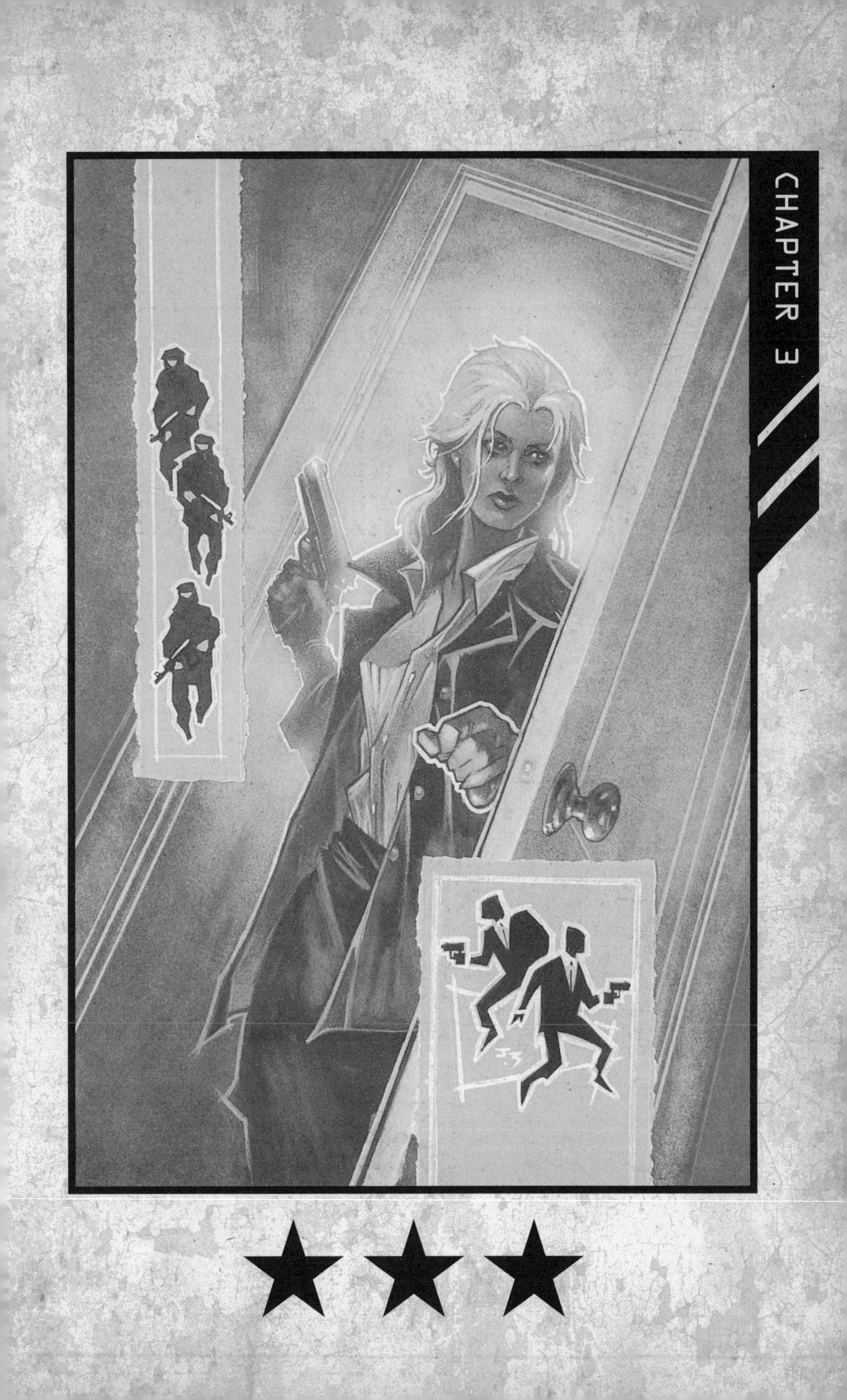

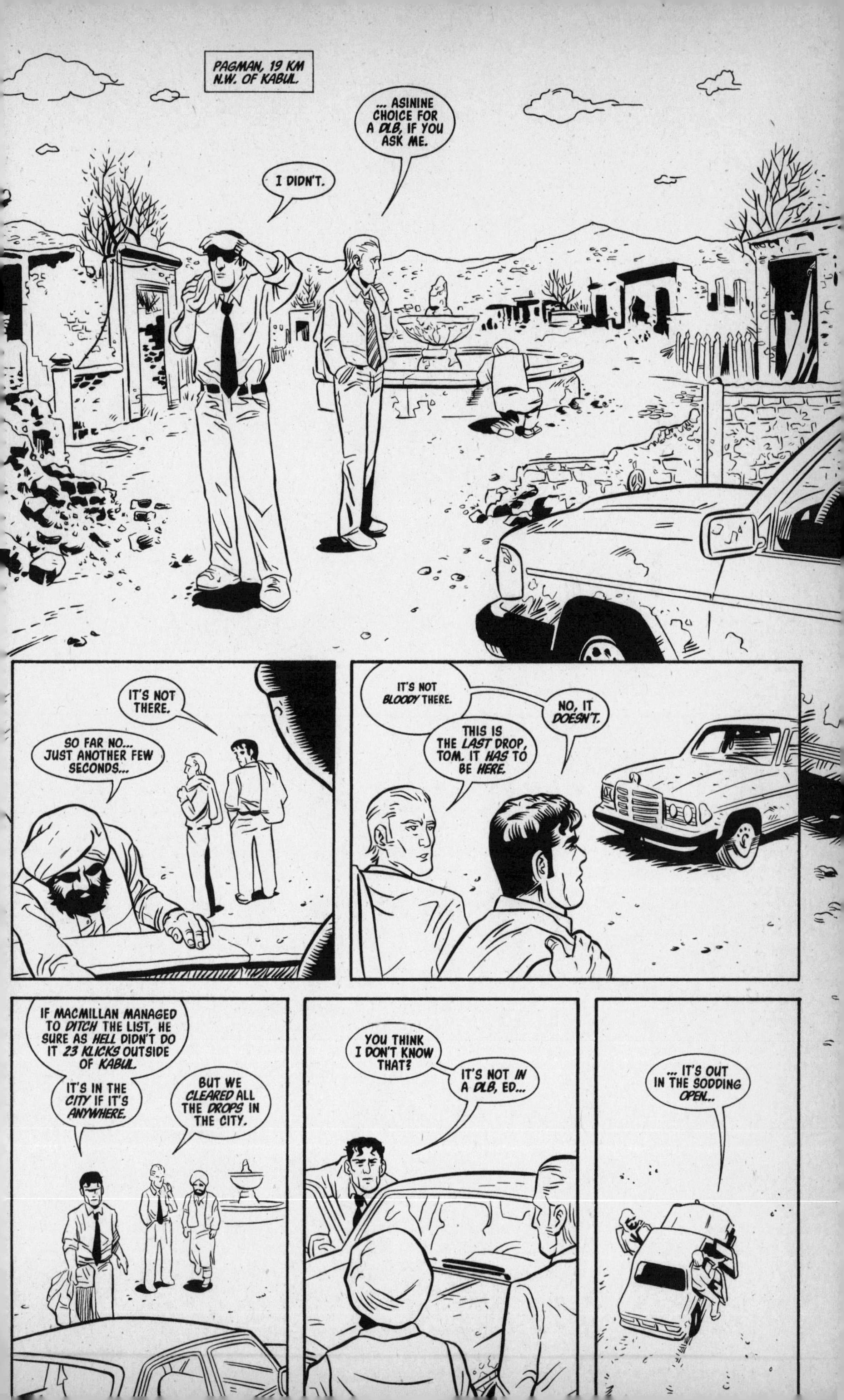
PAGMAN, 19 KM N.W. OF KABUL.
... ASININE CHOICE FOR A DLB, IF YOU ASK ME.
I DIDN'T.
IT'S NOT THERE.
SO FAR NO... JUST ANOTHER FEW SECONDS...
IT'S NOT BLOODY THERE.
NO, IT DOESN'T.
THIS IS THE LAST DROP, TOM. IT HAS TO BE HERE.
IF MACMILLAN MANAGED TO DITCH THE LIST, HE SURE AS HELL DIDN'T DO IT 23 KLICKS OUTSIDE OF KABUL.
IT'S IN THE CITY IF IT'S ANYWHERE.
BUT WE CLEARED ALL THE DROPS IN THE CITY.
YOU THINK I DON'T KNOW THAT?
IT'S NOT IN A DLB, ED...
... IT'S OUT IN THE SODDING OPEN...

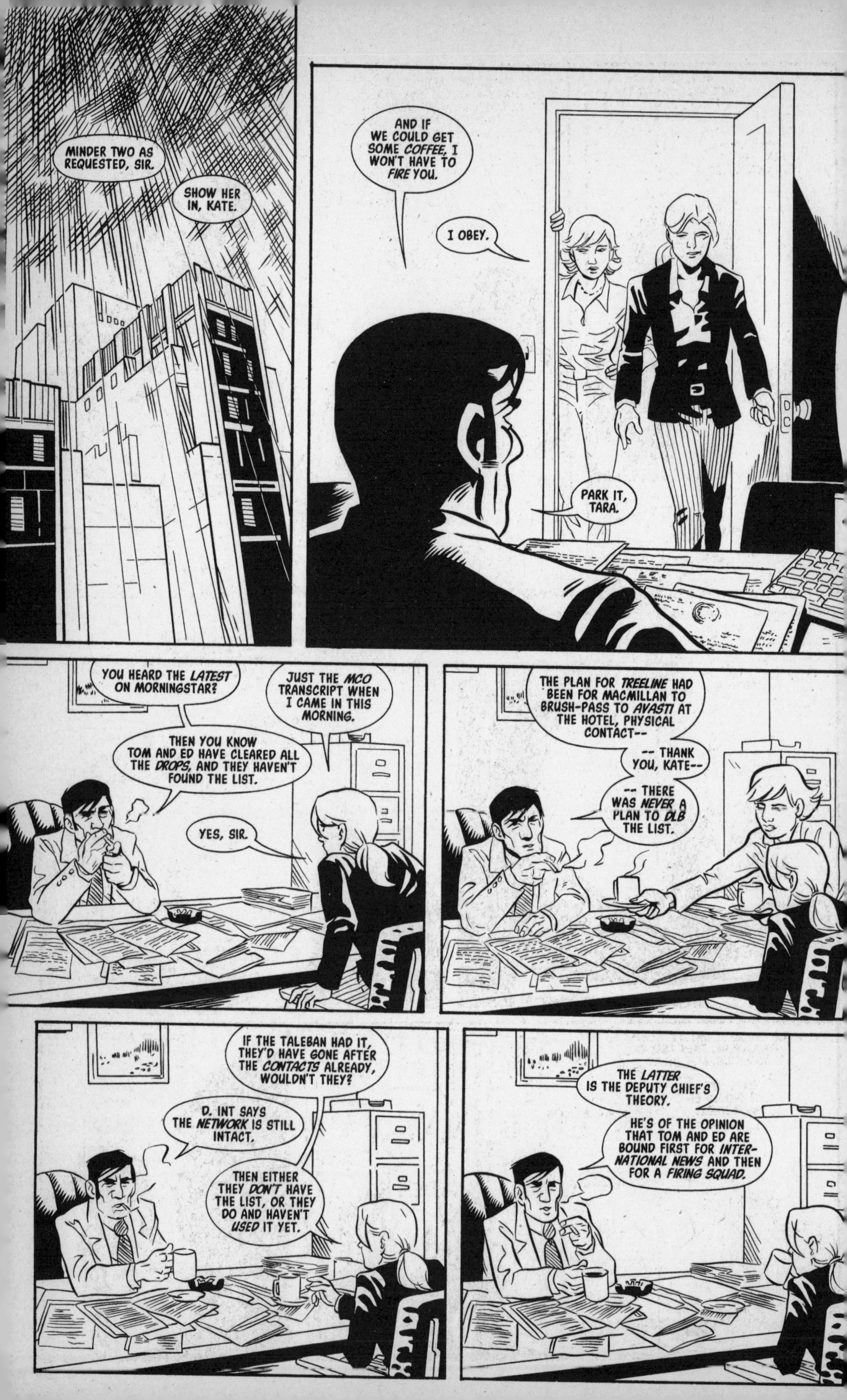
MINDER TWO AS REQUESTED, SIR.
SHOW HER IN, KATE.
AND IF WE COULD GET SOME *COFFEE*, I WON'T HAVE TO *FIRE* YOU.
I OBEY.
PARK IT, TARA.
YOU HEARD THE *LATEST* ON MORNINGSTAR?
JUST THE *MCO* TRANSCRIPT WHEN I CAME IN THIS MORNING.
THEN YOU KNOW TOM AND ED HAVE CLEARED ALL THE *DROPS*, AND THEY HAVEN'T FOUND THE LIST.
YES, SIR.
THE PLAN FOR *TREELINE* HAD BEEN FOR MACMILLAN TO BRUSH-PASS TO *AVASTI* AT THE HOTEL, PHYSICAL CONTACT--
-- THANK YOU, KATE--
-- THERE WAS *NEVER* A PLAN TO *DLB* THE LIST.
IF THE TALEBAN HAD IT, THEY'D HAVE GONE AFTER THE *CONTACTS* ALREADY, WOULDN'T THEY?
D. INT SAYS THE *NETWORK* IS STILL INTACT.
THEN EITHER THEY *DON'T* HAVE THE LIST, OR THEY DO AND HAVEN'T *USED* IT YET.
THE *LATTER* IS THE DEPUTY CHIEF'S THEORY.
HE'S OF THE OPINION THAT TOM AND ED ARE BOUND FIRST FOR *INTERNATIONAL NEWS* AND THEN FOR A *FIRING SQUAD*.

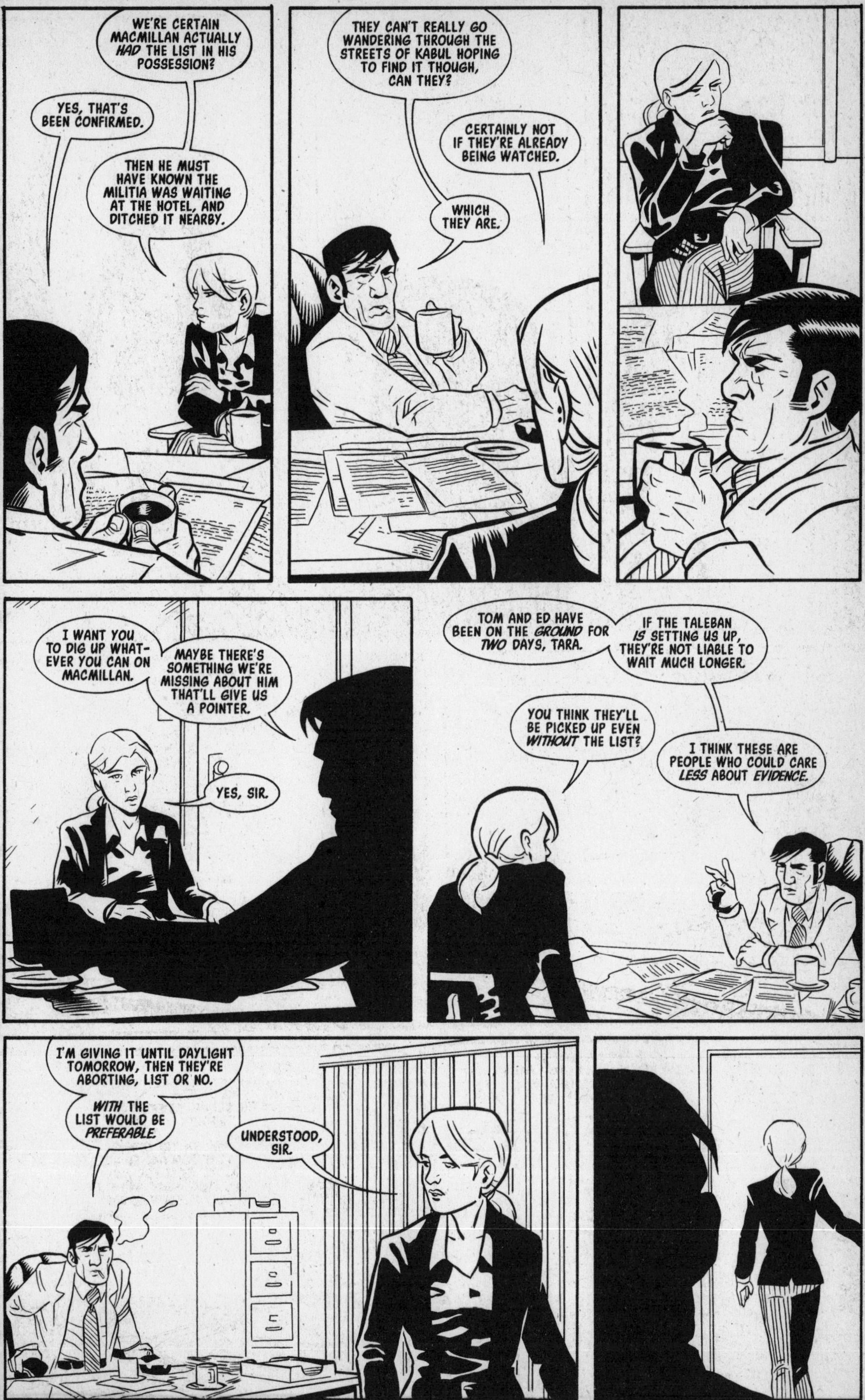
WE'RE CERTAIN MACMILLAN ACTUALLY *HAD* THE LIST IN HIS POSSESSION?
YES, THAT'S BEEN CONFIRMED.
THEN HE MUST HAVE KNOWN THE MILITIA WAS WAITING AT THE HOTEL, AND DITCHED IT NEARBY.
THEY CAN'T REALLY GO WANDERING THROUGH THE STREETS OF KABUL HOPING TO FIND IT THOUGH, CAN THEY?
CERTAINLY NOT IF THEY'RE ALREADY BEING WATCHED.
WHICH THEY ARE.
I WANT YOU TO DIG UP WHATEVER YOU CAN ON MACMILLAN.
MAYBE THERE'S SOMETHING WE'RE MISSING ABOUT HIM THAT'LL GIVE US A POINTER.
YES, SIR.
TOM AND ED HAVE BEEN ON THE *GROUND* FOR *TWO* DAYS, TARA.
IF THE TALEBAN *IS* SETTING US UP, THEY'RE NOT LIABLE TO WAIT MUCH LONGER.
YOU THINK THEY'LL BE PICKED UP EVEN *WITHOUT* THE LIST?
I THINK THESE ARE PEOPLE WHO COULD CARE *LESS* ABOUT *EVIDENCE*.
I'M GIVING IT UNTIL DAYLIGHT TOMORROW, THEN THEY'RE ABORTING, LIST OR NO.
WITH THE LIST WOULD BE *PREFERABLE*.
UNDERSTOOD, SIR.

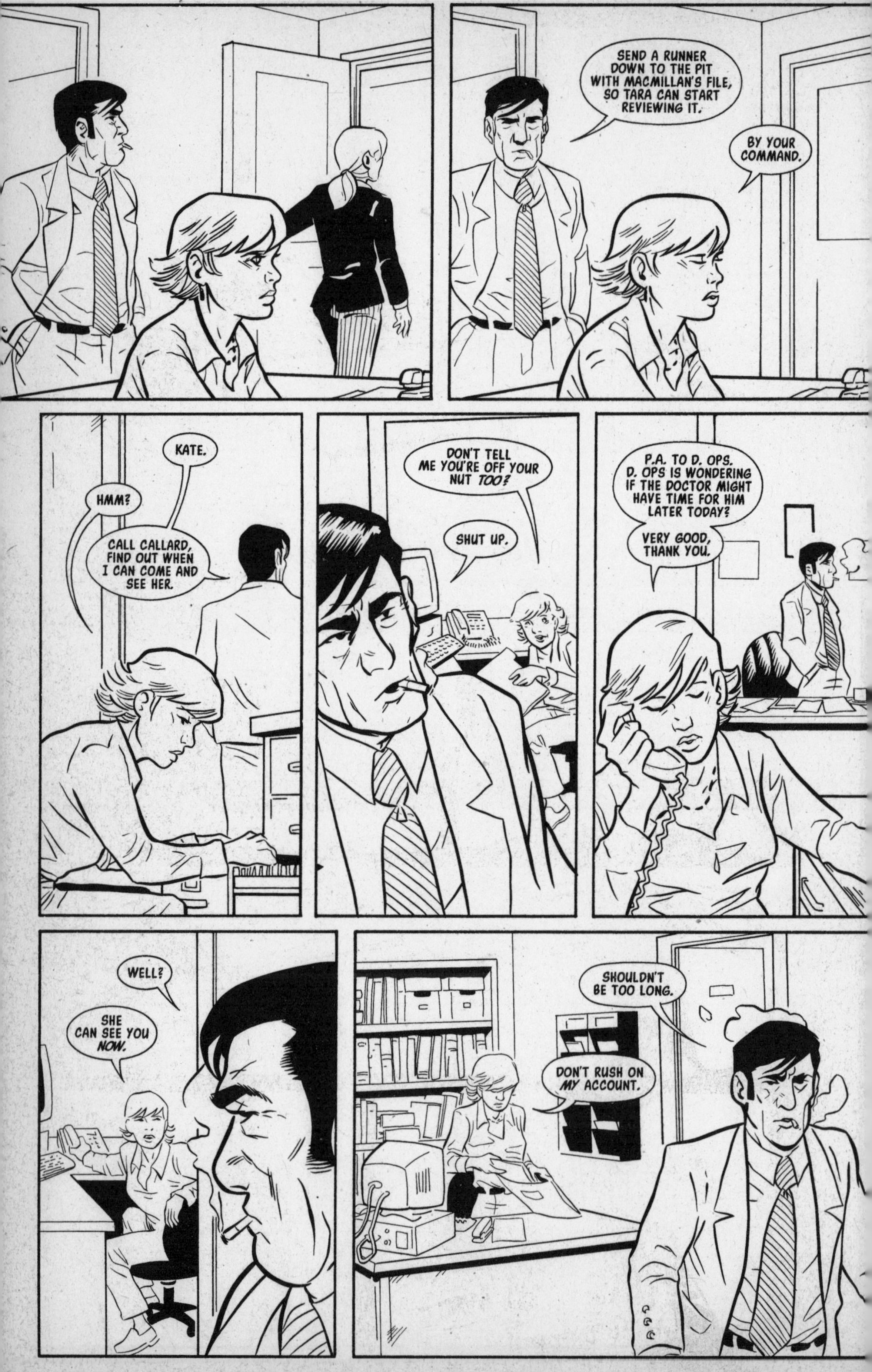

SEND A RUNNER DOWN TO THE PIT WITH MACMILLAN'S FILE, SO TARA CAN START REVIEWING IT.
BY YOUR COMMAND.
KATE.
HMM?
CALL CALLARD, FIND OUT WHEN I CAN COME AND SEE HER.
DON'T TELL ME YOU'RE OFF YOUR NUT *TOO*?
SHUT UP.
P.A. TO D. OPS. D. OPS IS WONDERING IF THE DOCTOR MIGHT HAVE TIME FOR HIM LATER TODAY?
VERY GOOD, THANK YOU.
WELL?
SHE CAN SEE YOU *NOW*.
SHOULDN'T BE TOO LONG.
DON'T RUSH ON *MY* ACCOUNT.

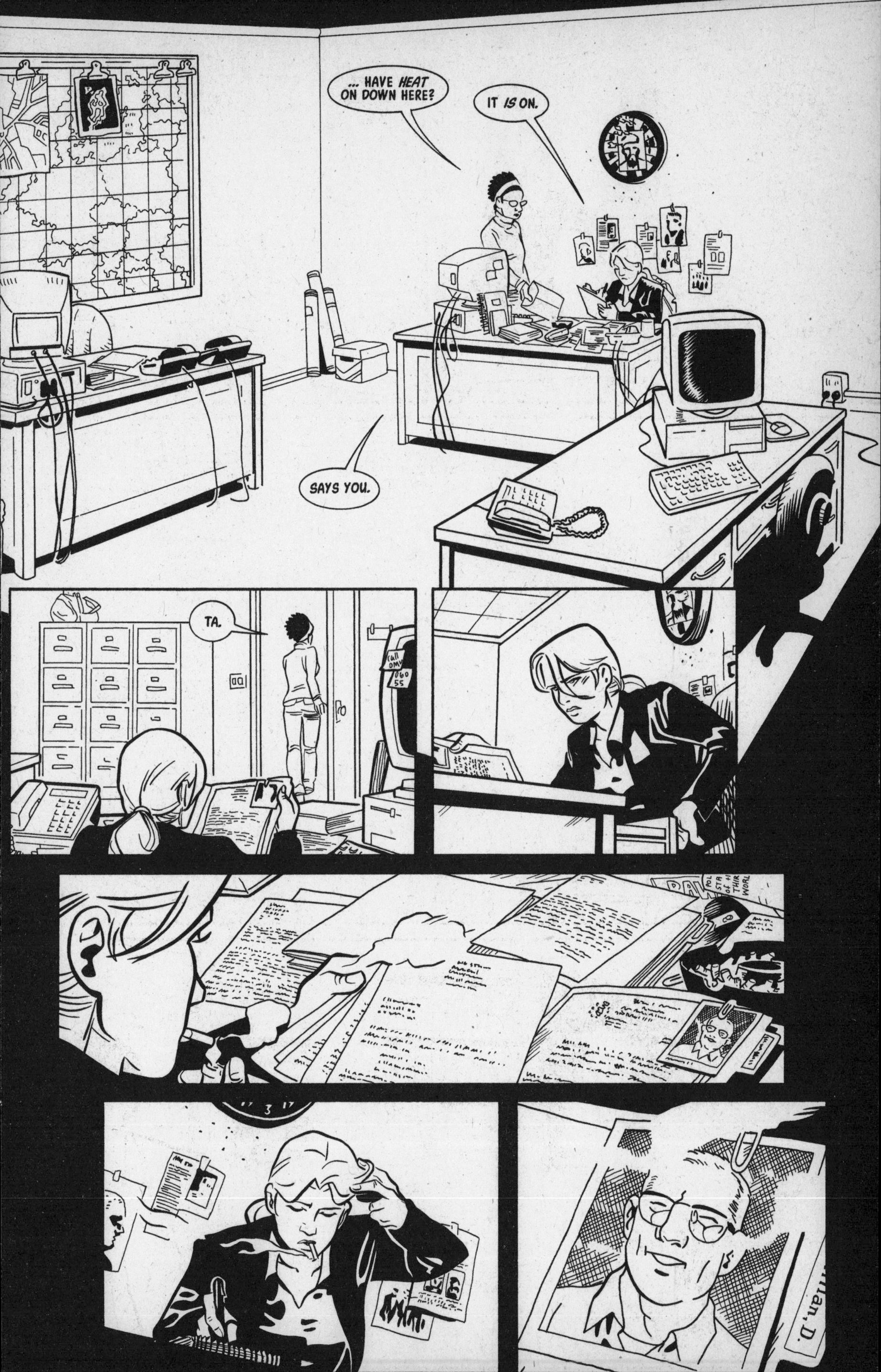
... HAVE HEAT ON DOWN HERE?
IT IS ON.
SAYS YOU.
TA.

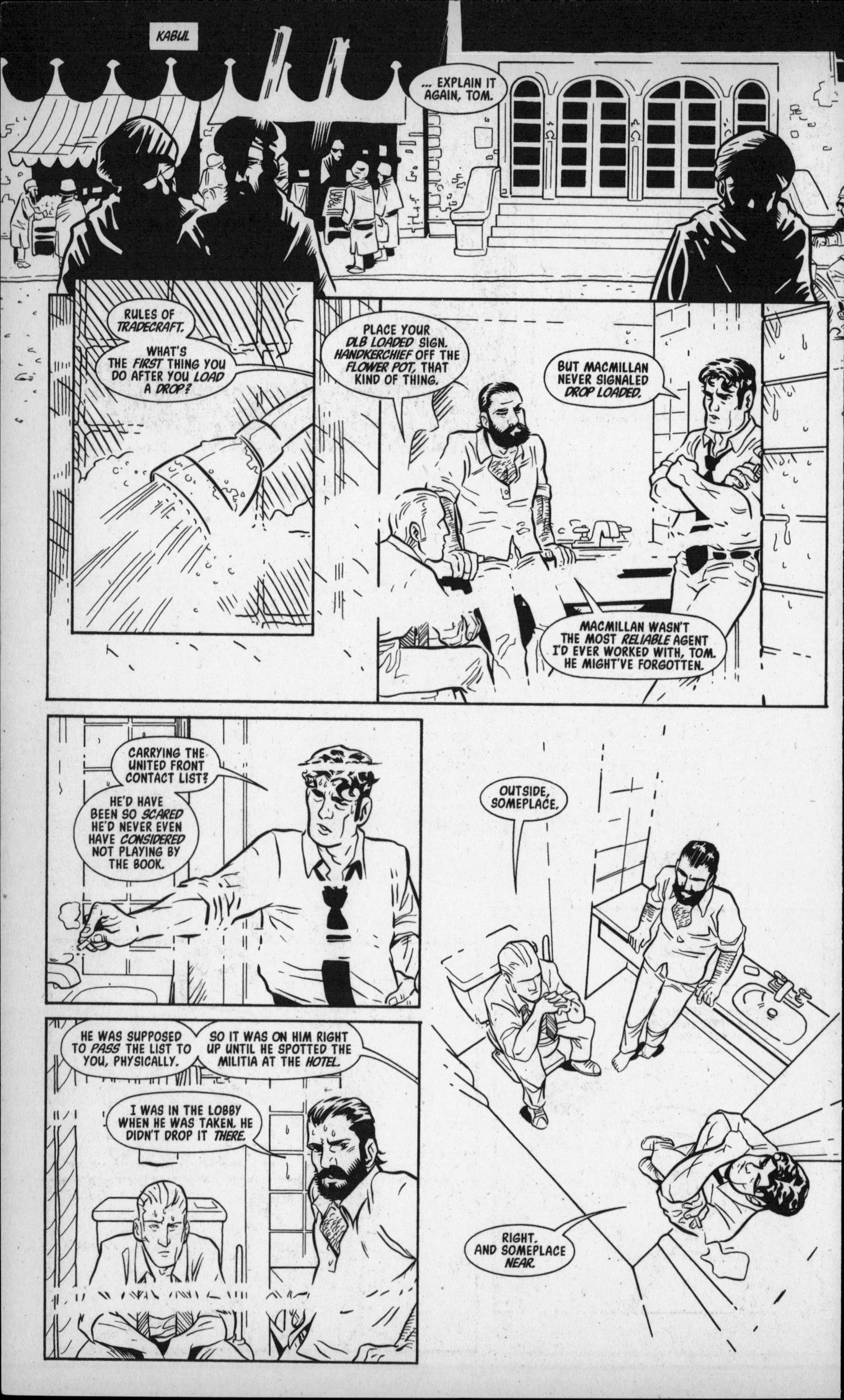

KABUL
... EXPLAIN IT AGAIN, TOM.
RULES OF TRADECRAFT.
WHAT'S THE FIRST THING YOU DO AFTER YOU LOAD A DROP?
PLACE YOUR DLB LOADED SIGN. HANDKERCHIEF OFF THE FLOWER POT, THAT KIND OF THING.
BUT MACMILLAN NEVER SIGNALED DROP LOADED.
MACMILLAN WASN'T THE MOST RELIABLE AGENT I'D EVER WORKED WITH, TOM. HE MIGHT'VE FORGOTTEN.
CARRYING THE UNITED FRONT CONTACT LIST?
HE'D HAVE BEEN SO SCARED HE'D NEVER EVEN HAVE CONSIDERED NOT PLAYING BY THE BOOK.
HE WAS SUPPOSED TO PASS THE LIST TO YOU, PHYSICALLY.
SO IT WAS ON HIM RIGHT UP UNTIL HE SPOTTED THE MILITIA AT THE HOTEL.
I WAS IN THE LOBBY WHEN HE WAS TAKEN. HE DIDN'T DROP IT THERE.
OUTSIDE, SOMEPLACE.
RIGHT. AND SOMEPLACE NEAR.

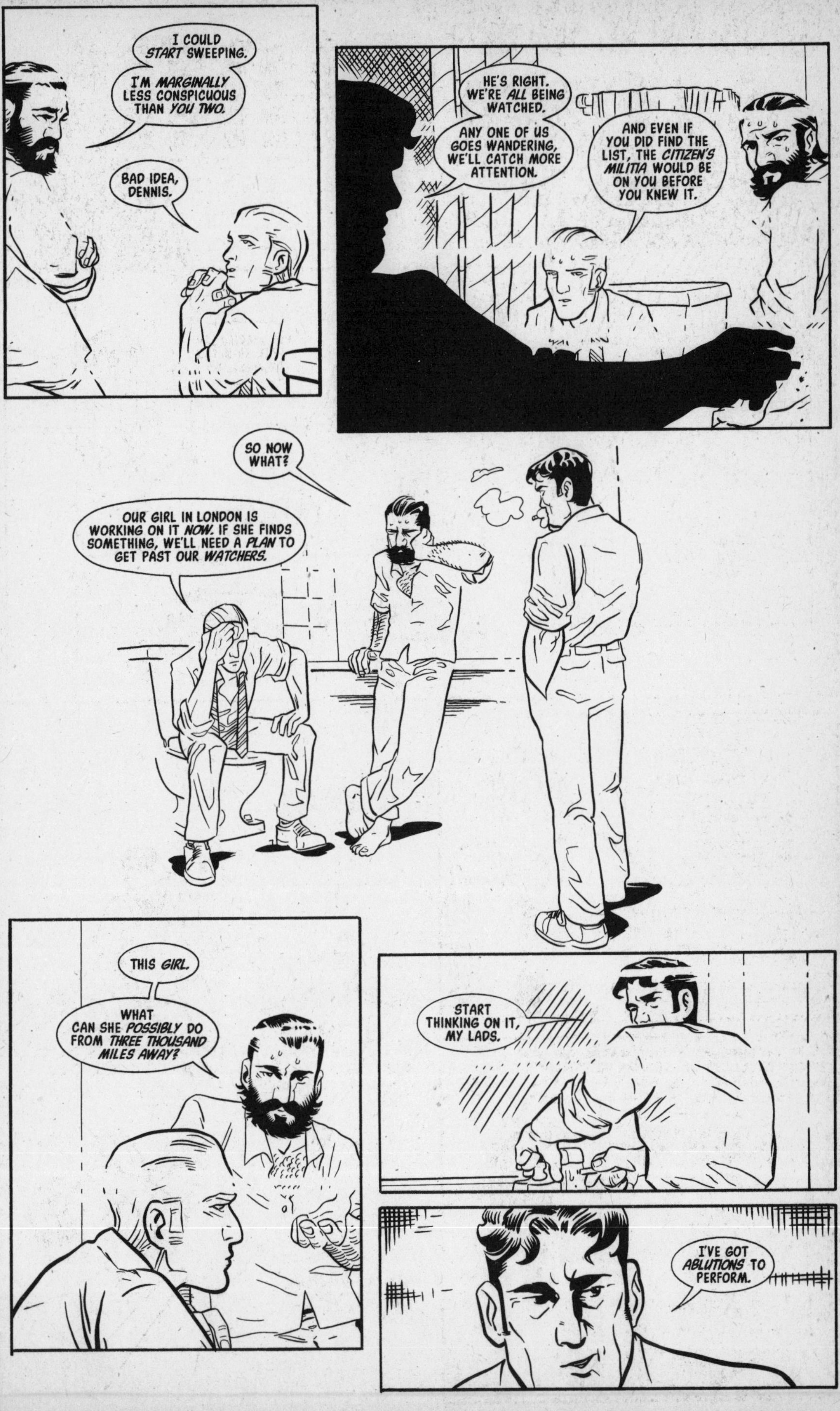
I COULD START SWEEPING.
I'M MARGINALLY LESS CONSPICUOUS THAN YOU TWO.
BAD IDEA, DENNIS.
HE'S RIGHT. WE'RE ALL BEING WATCHED.
ANY ONE OF US GOES WANDERING, WE'LL CATCH MORE ATTENTION.
AND EVEN IF YOU DID FIND THE LIST, THE CITIZEN'S MILITIA WOULD BE ON YOU BEFORE YOU KNEW IT.
SO NOW WHAT?
OUR GIRL IN LONDON IS WORKING ON IT NOW. IF SHE FINDS SOMETHING, WE'LL NEED A PLAN TO GET PAST OUR WATCHERS.
THIS GIRL.
WHAT CAN SHE POSSIBLY DO FROM THREE THOUSAND MILES AWAY?
START THINKING ON IT, MY LADS.
I'VE GOT ABLUTIONS TO PERFORM.

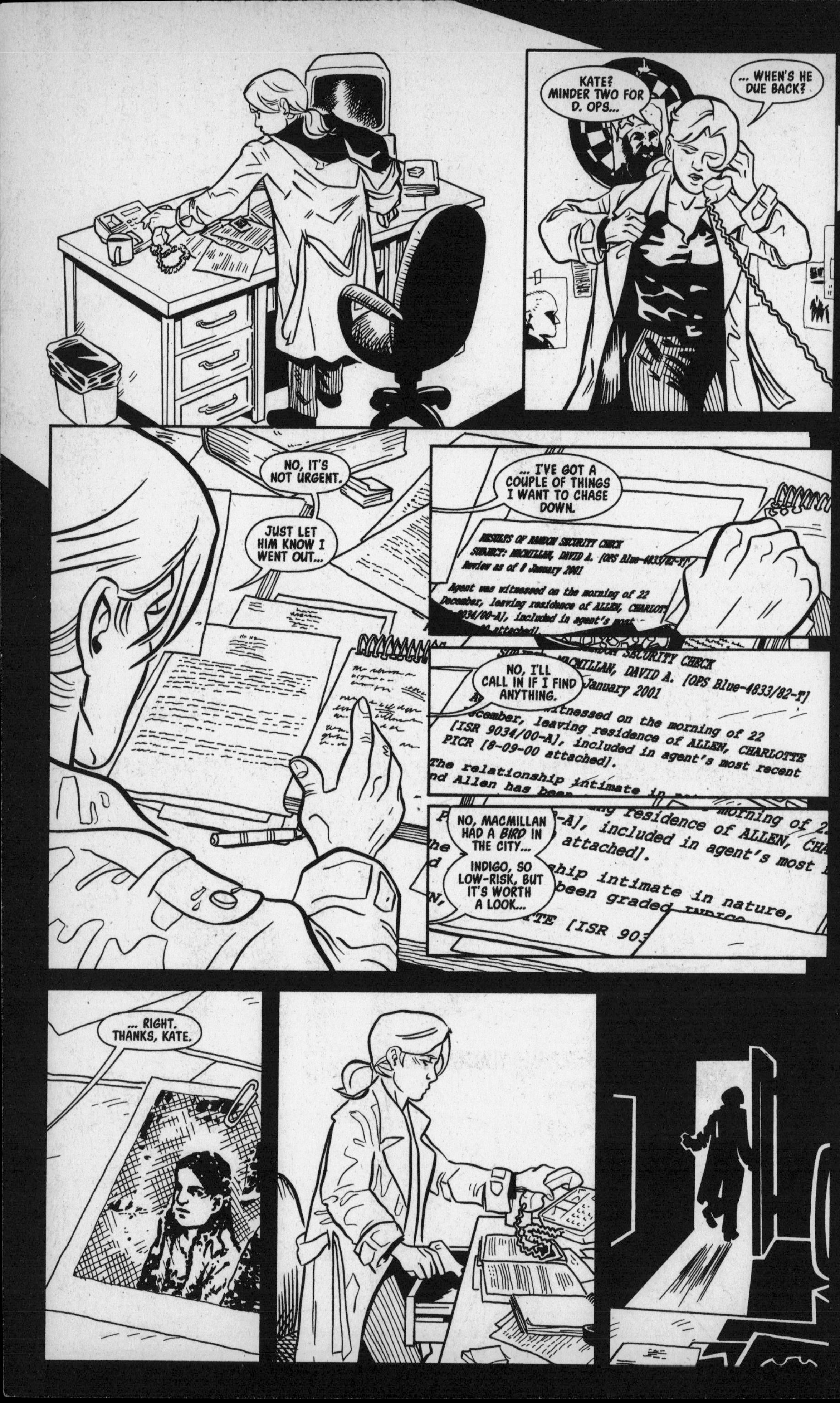

KATE? MINDER TWO FOR D. OPS...
... WHEN'S HE DUE BACK?
NO, IT'S NOT URGENT.
JUST LET HIM KNOW I WENT OUT...
... I'VE GOT A COUPLE OF THINGS I WANT TO CHASE DOWN.
RESULTS OF RANDOM SECURITY CHECK
SUBJECT: MACMILLAN, DAVID A. [OPS Blue-4833/82-T]
Review as of 8 January 2001
Agent was witnessed on the morning of 22
NO, I'LL CALL IN IF I FIND ANYTHING.
[ISR 9034/00-A], included in agent's most recent
PICR [8-09-00 attached].
NO, MACMILLAN HAD A *BIRD* IN THE CITY...
INDIGO, SO LOW-RISK, BUT IT'S WORTH A LOOK...
... RIGHT. THANKS, KATE.

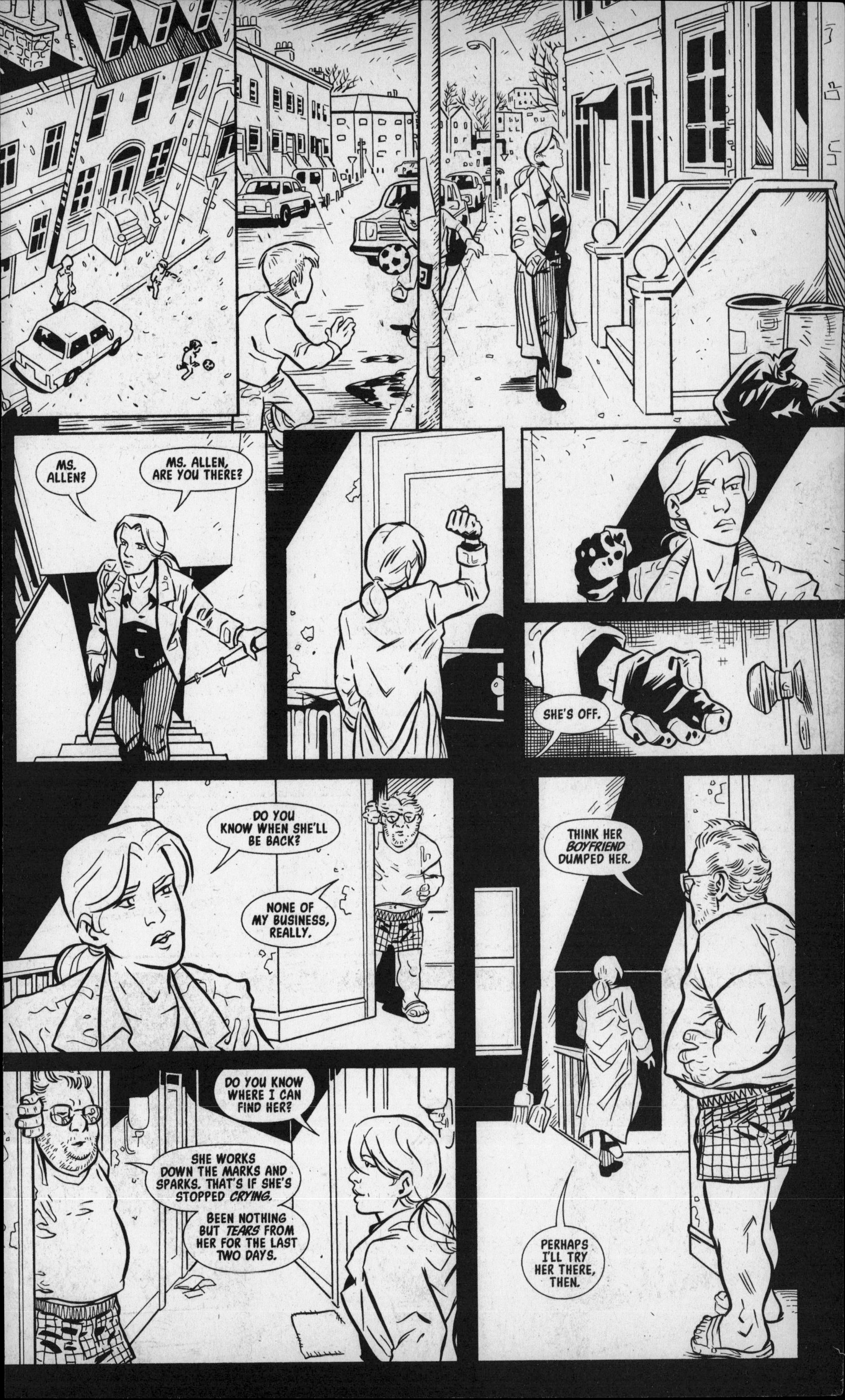
MS. ALLEN?
MS. ALLEN, ARE YOU THERE?
SHE'S OFF.
DO YOU KNOW WHEN SHE'LL BE BACK?
NONE OF MY BUSINESS, REALLY.
THINK HER BOYFRIEND DUMPED HER.
DO YOU KNOW WHERE I CAN FIND HER?
SHE WORKS DOWN THE MARKS AND SPARKS. THAT'S IF SHE'S STOPPED CRYING.
BEEN NOTHING BUT TEARS FROM HER FOR THE LAST TWO DAYS.
PERHAPS I'LL TRY HER THERE, THEN.

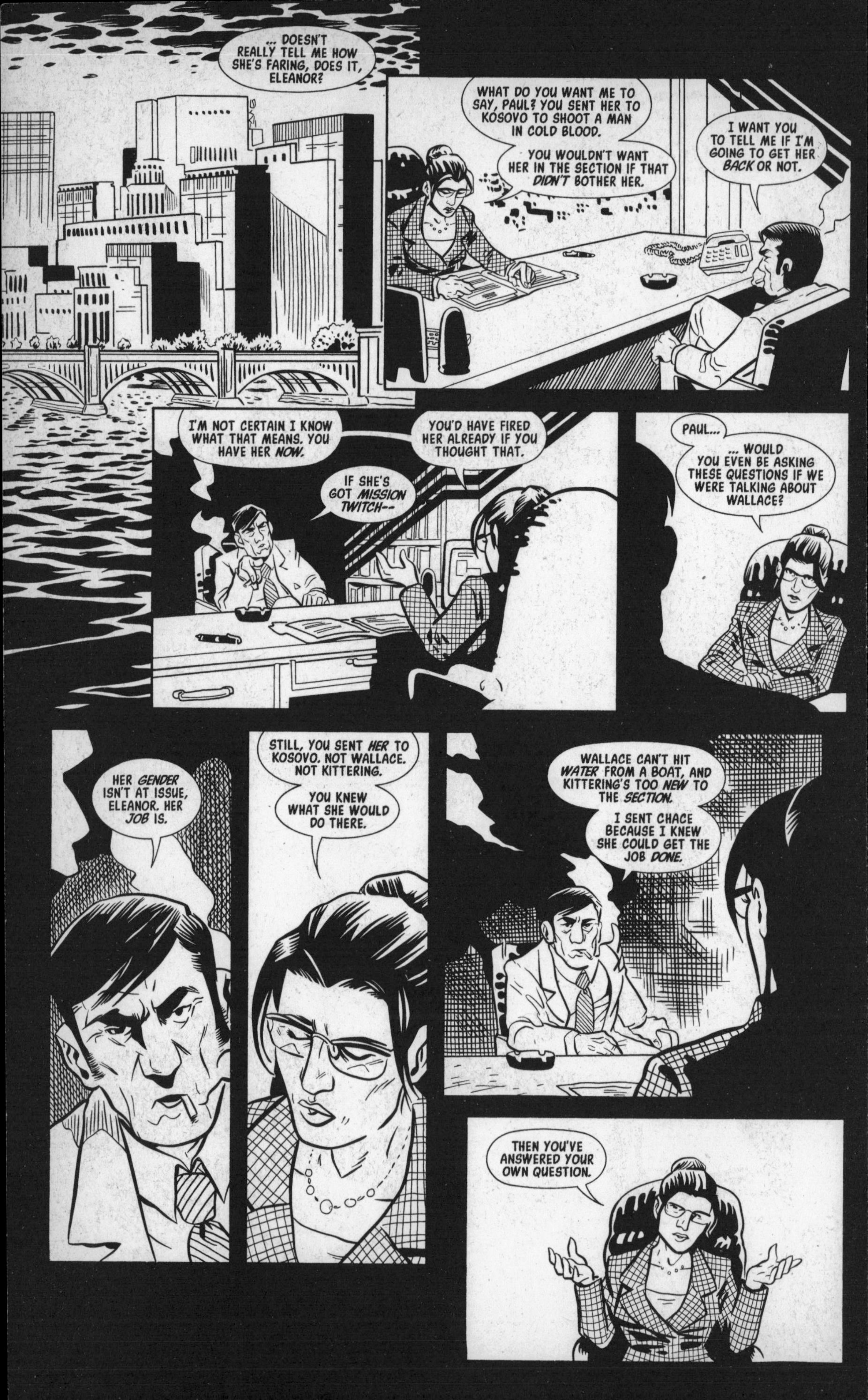
... DOESN'T REALLY TELL ME HOW SHE'S FARING, DOES IT, ELEANOR?
WHAT DO YOU WANT ME TO SAY, PAUL? YOU SENT HER TO KOSOVO TO SHOOT A MAN IN COLD BLOOD.
YOU WOULDN'T WANT HER IN THE SECTION IF THAT *DIDN'T* BOTHER HER.
I WANT YOU TO TELL ME IF I'M GOING TO GET HER *BACK* OR NOT.
I'M NOT CERTAIN I KNOW WHAT THAT MEANS. YOU HAVE HER *NOW*.
YOU'D HAVE FIRED HER ALREADY IF YOU THOUGHT THAT.
IF SHE'S GOT *MISSION TWITCH*--
PAUL...
... WOULD YOU EVEN BE ASKING THESE QUESTIONS IF WE WERE TALKING ABOUT WALLACE?
HER *GENDER* ISN'T AT ISSUE, ELEANOR. HER *JOB* IS.
STILL, YOU SENT *HER* TO KOSOVO. NOT WALLACE. NOT KITTERING.
YOU KNEW WHAT SHE WOULD DO THERE.
WALLACE CAN'T HIT *WATER* FROM A BOAT, AND KITTERING'S TOO *NEW* TO THE *SECTION*.
I SENT CHACE BECAUSE I KNEW SHE COULD GET THE JOB *DONE*.
THEN YOU'VE ANSWERED YOUR OWN QUESTION.

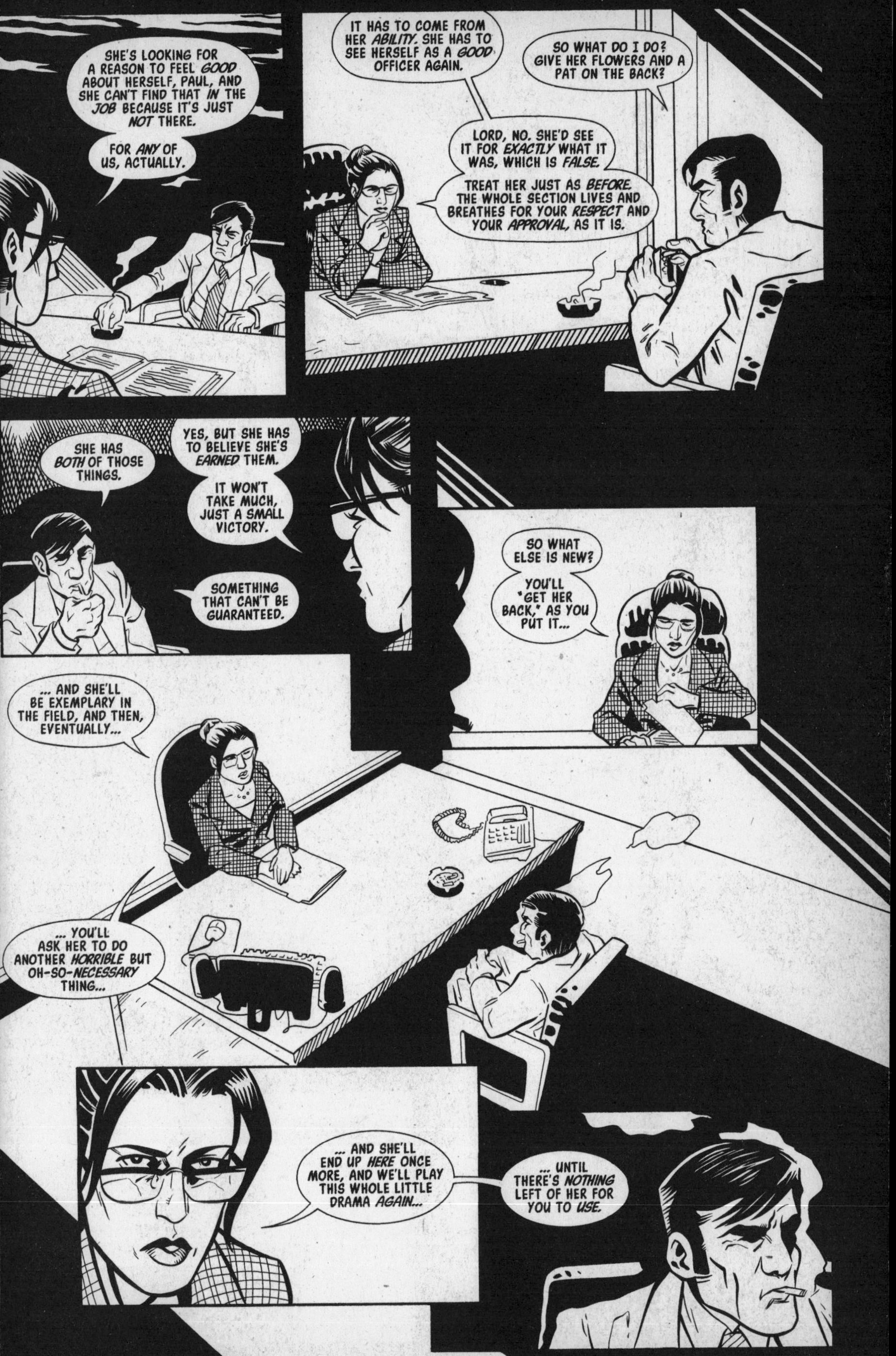
SHE'S LOOKING FOR A REASON TO FEEL GOOD ABOUT HERSELF, PAUL, AND SHE CAN'T FIND THAT IN THE JOB BECAUSE IT'S JUST NOT THERE.
FOR ANY OF US, ACTUALLY.
IT HAS TO COME FROM HER ABILITY. SHE HAS TO SEE HERSELF AS A GOOD OFFICER AGAIN.
SO WHAT DO I DO? GIVE HER FLOWERS AND A PAT ON THE BACK?
LORD, NO. SHE'D SEE IT FOR EXACTLY WHAT IT WAS, WHICH IS FALSE.
TREAT HER JUST AS BEFORE. THE WHOLE SECTION LIVES AND BREATHES FOR YOUR RESPECT AND YOUR APPROVAL, AS IT IS.
SHE HAS BOTH OF THOSE THINGS.
YES, BUT SHE HAS TO BELIEVE SHE'S EARNED THEM.
IT WON'T TAKE MUCH, JUST A SMALL VICTORY.
SOMETHING THAT CAN'T BE GUARANTEED.
SO WHAT ELSE IS NEW?
YOU'LL "GET HER BACK," AS YOU PUT IT...
... AND SHE'LL BE EXEMPLARY IN THE FIELD, AND THEN, EVENTUALLY...
... YOU'LL ASK HER TO DO ANOTHER HORRIBLE BUT OH-SO-NECESSARY THING...
... AND SHE'LL END UP HERE ONCE MORE, AND WE'LL PLAY THIS WHOLE LITTLE DRAMA AGAIN...
... UNTIL THERE'S NOTHING LEFT OF HER FOR YOU TO USE.

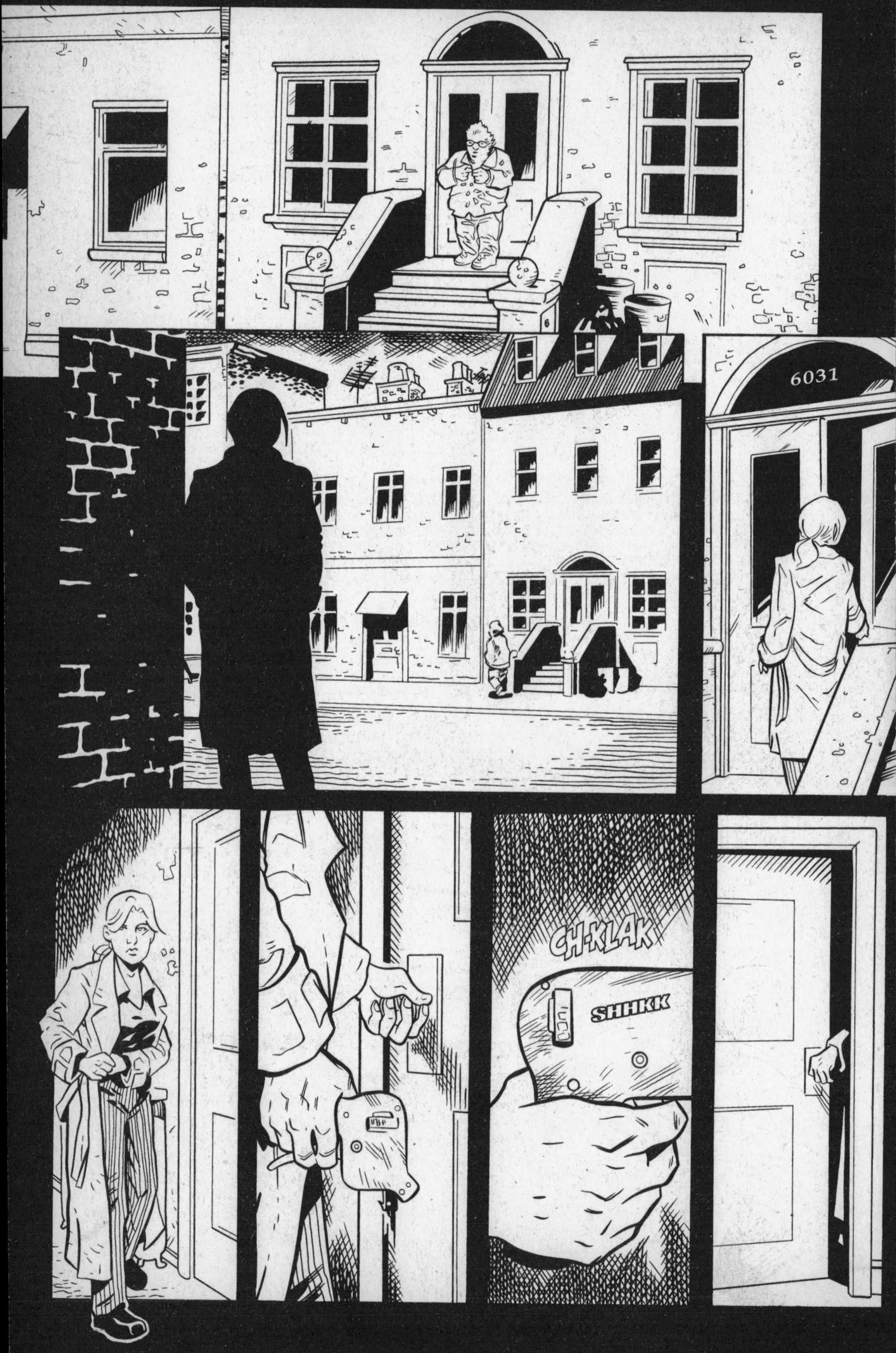
6031
CH-KLAK
SHHKK

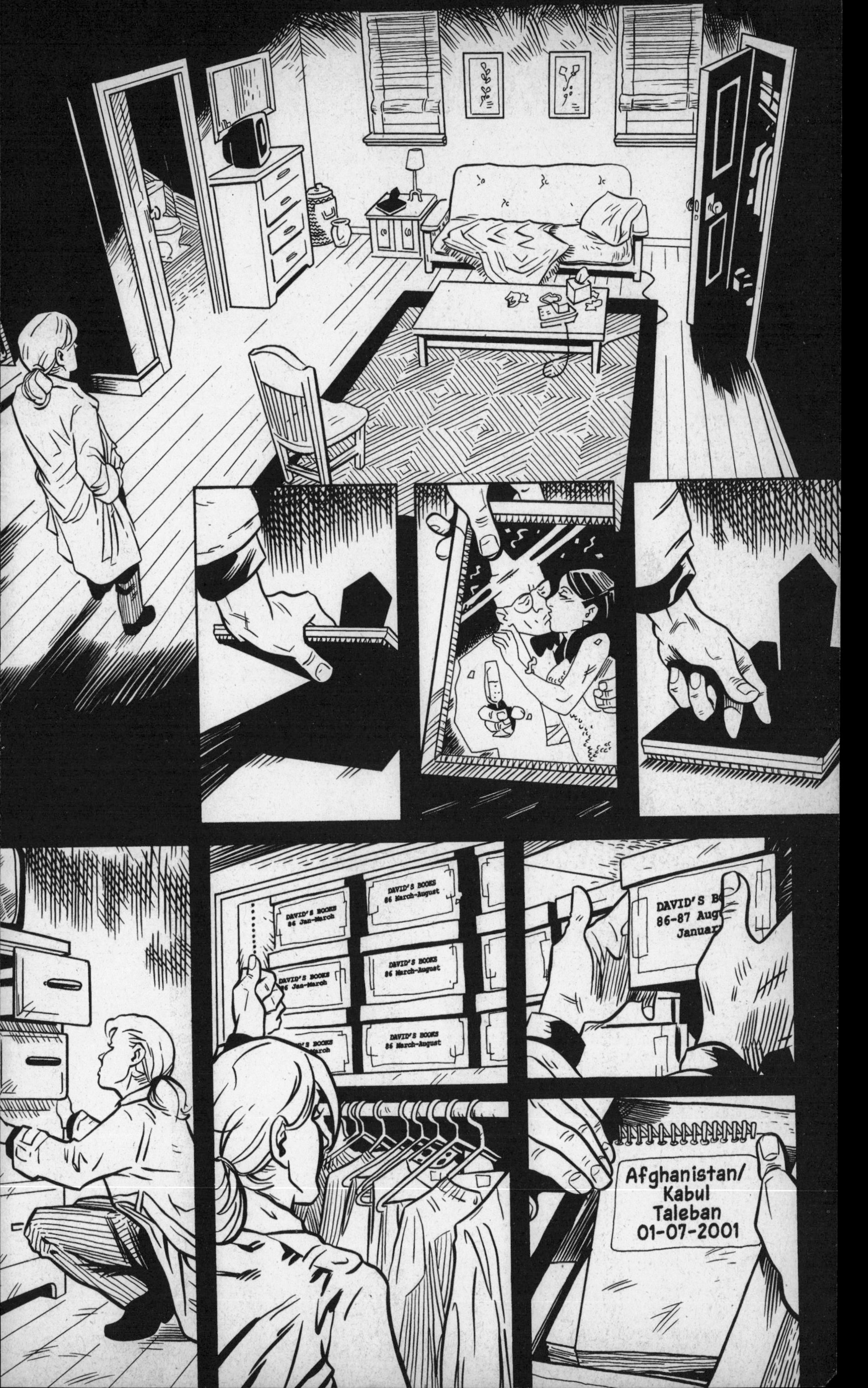
DAVID'S BOOKS
86 Jan-March
DAVID'S BOOKS
86 March-August
DAVID'S BOOKS
86 March-August
DAVID'S BOOKS
86 March-August
DAVID'S B
86-87 Aug
Januar
Afghanistan/
Kabul
Taleban
01-07-2001

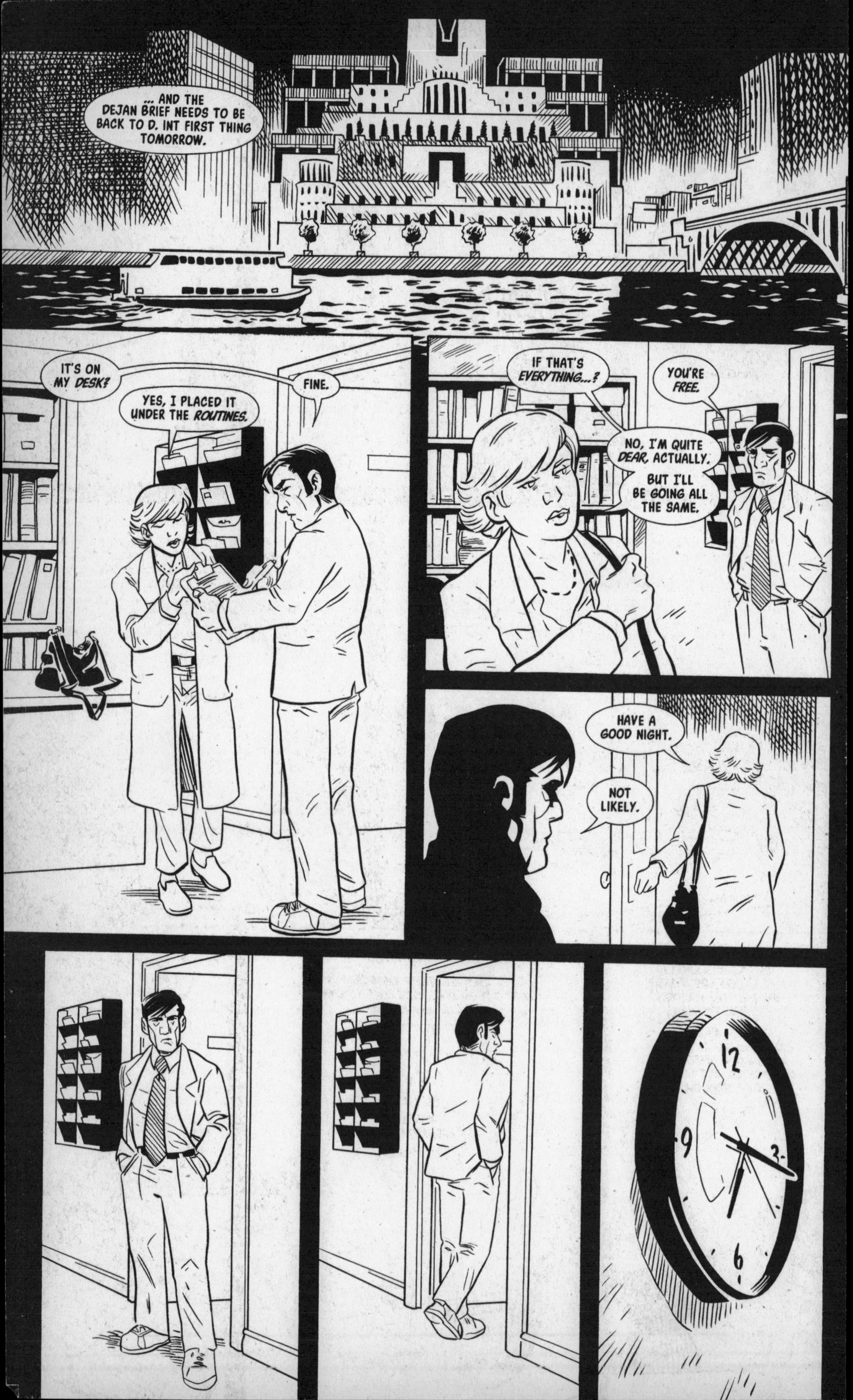

... AND THE DEJAN BRIEF NEEDS TO BE BACK TO D. INT FIRST THING TOMORROW.
IT'S ON MY DESK?
YES, I PLACED IT UNDER THE ROUTINES.
FINE.
IF THAT'S EVERYTHING...?
YOU'RE FREE.
NO, I'M QUITE DEAR, ACTUALLY.
BUT I'LL BE GOING ALL THE SAME.
HAVE A GOOD NIGHT.
NOT LIKELY.
12
9
3
6

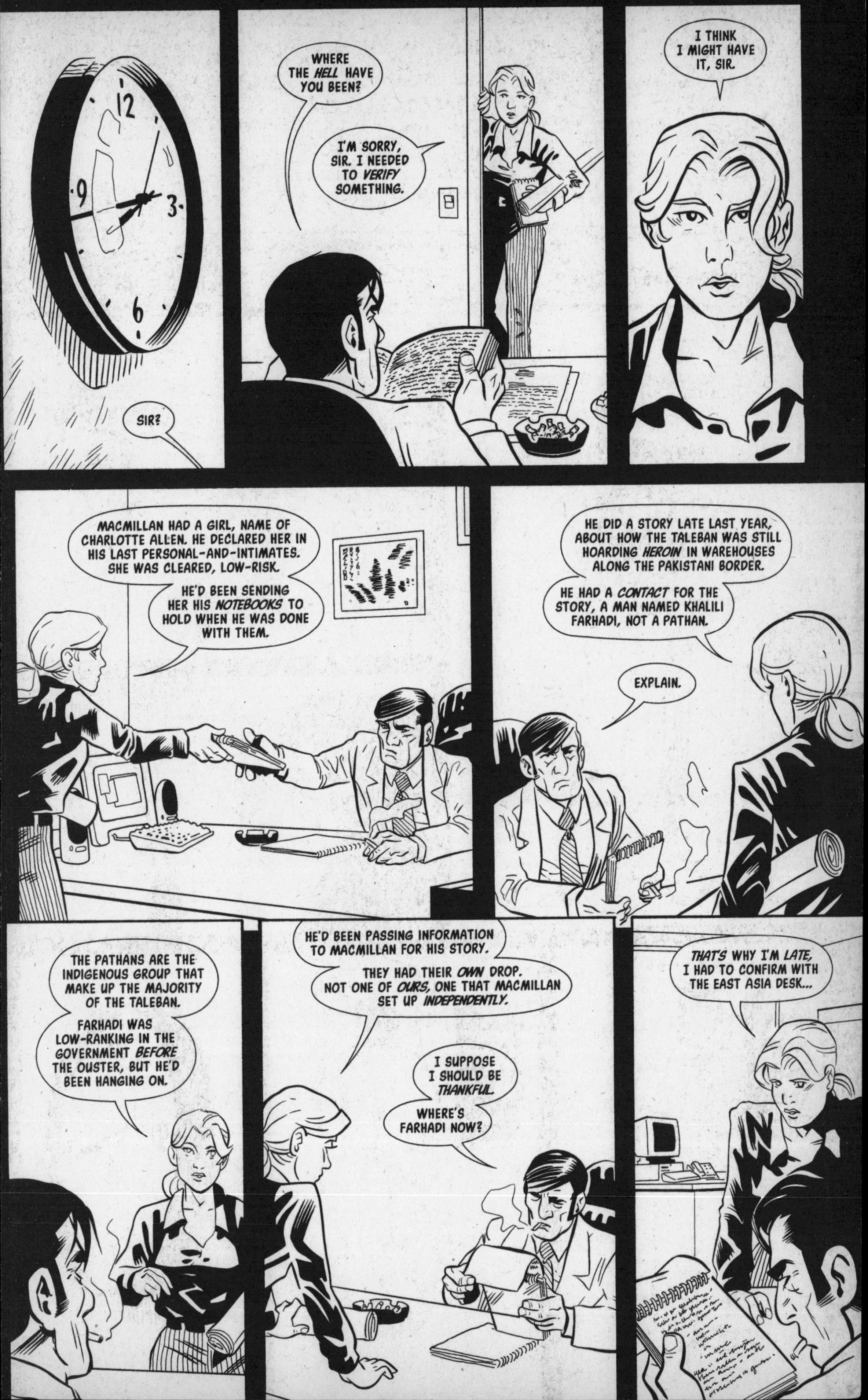
SIR?
WHERE THE HELL HAVE YOU BEEN?
I'M SORRY, SIR. I NEEDED TO VERIFY SOMETHING.
I THINK I MIGHT HAVE IT, SIR.
MACMILLAN HAD A GIRL, NAME OF CHARLOTTE ALLEN. HE DECLARED HER IN HIS LAST PERSONAL-AND-INTIMATES. SHE WAS CLEARED, LOW-RISK.
HE'D BEEN SENDING HER HIS NOTEBOOKS TO HOLD WHEN HE WAS DONE WITH THEM.
HE DID A STORY LATE LAST YEAR, ABOUT HOW THE TALEBAN WAS STILL HOARDING HEROIN IN WAREHOUSES ALONG THE PAKISTANI BORDER.
HE HAD A CONTACT FOR THE STORY, A MAN NAMED KHALILI FARHADI, NOT A PATHAN.
EXPLAIN.
THE PATHANS ARE THE INDIGENOUS GROUP THAT MAKE UP THE MAJORITY OF THE TALEBAN.
FARHADI WAS LOW-RANKING IN THE GOVERNMENT BEFORE THE OUSTER, BUT HE'D BEEN HANGING ON.
HE'D BEEN PASSING INFORMATION TO MACMILLAN FOR HIS STORY.
THEY HAD THEIR OWN DROP. NOT ONE OF OURS, ONE THAT MACMILLAN SET UP INDEPENDENTLY.
I SUPPOSE I SHOULD BE THANKFUL.
WHERE'S FARHADI NOW?
THAT'S WHY I'M LATE, I HAD TO CONFIRM WITH THE EAST ASIA DESK...

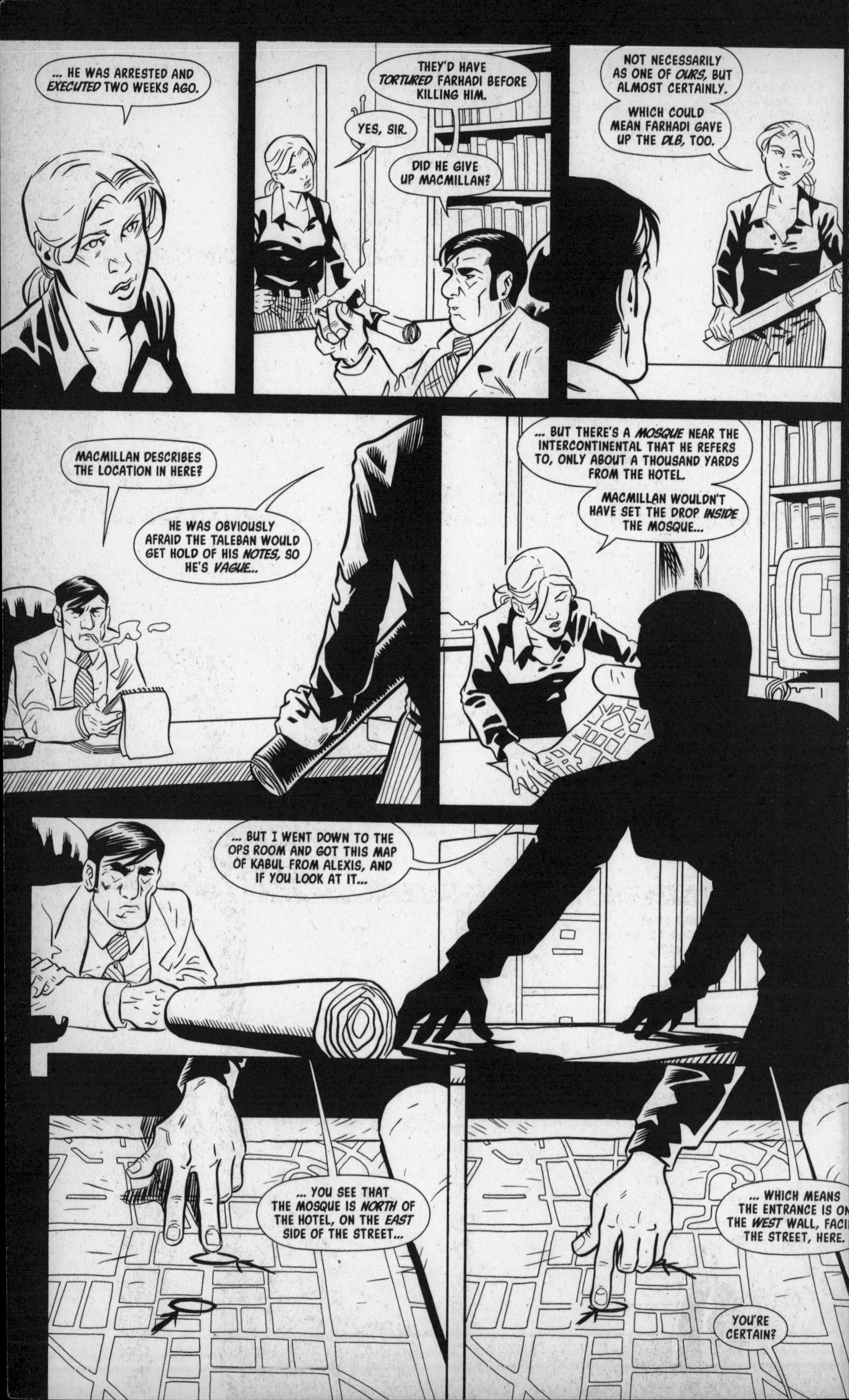
... HE WAS ARRESTED AND EXECUTED TWO WEEKS AGO.
THEY'D HAVE TORTURED FARHADI BEFORE KILLING HIM.
YES, SIR.
DID HE GIVE UP MACMILLAN?
NOT NECESSARILY AS ONE OF OURS, BUT ALMOST CERTAINLY.
WHICH COULD MEAN FARHADI GAVE UP THE DLB, TOO.
MACMILLAN DESCRIBES THE LOCATION IN HERE?
HE WAS OBVIOUSLY AFRAID THE TALEBAN WOULD GET HOLD OF HIS NOTES, SO HE'S VAGUE...
... BUT THERE'S A MOSQUE NEAR THE INTERCONTINENTAL THAT HE REFERS TO, ONLY ABOUT A THOUSAND YARDS FROM THE HOTEL.
MACMILLAN WOULDN'T HAVE SET THE DROP INSIDE THE MOSQUE...
... BUT I WENT DOWN TO THE OPS ROOM AND GOT THIS MAP OF KABUL FROM ALEXIS, AND IF YOU LOOK AT IT...
... YOU SEE THAT THE MOSQUE IS NORTH OF THE HOTEL, ON THE EAST SIDE OF THE STREET...
... WHICH MEANS THE ENTRANCE IS ON THE WEST WALL, FACI THE STREET, HERE.
YOU'RE CERTAIN?

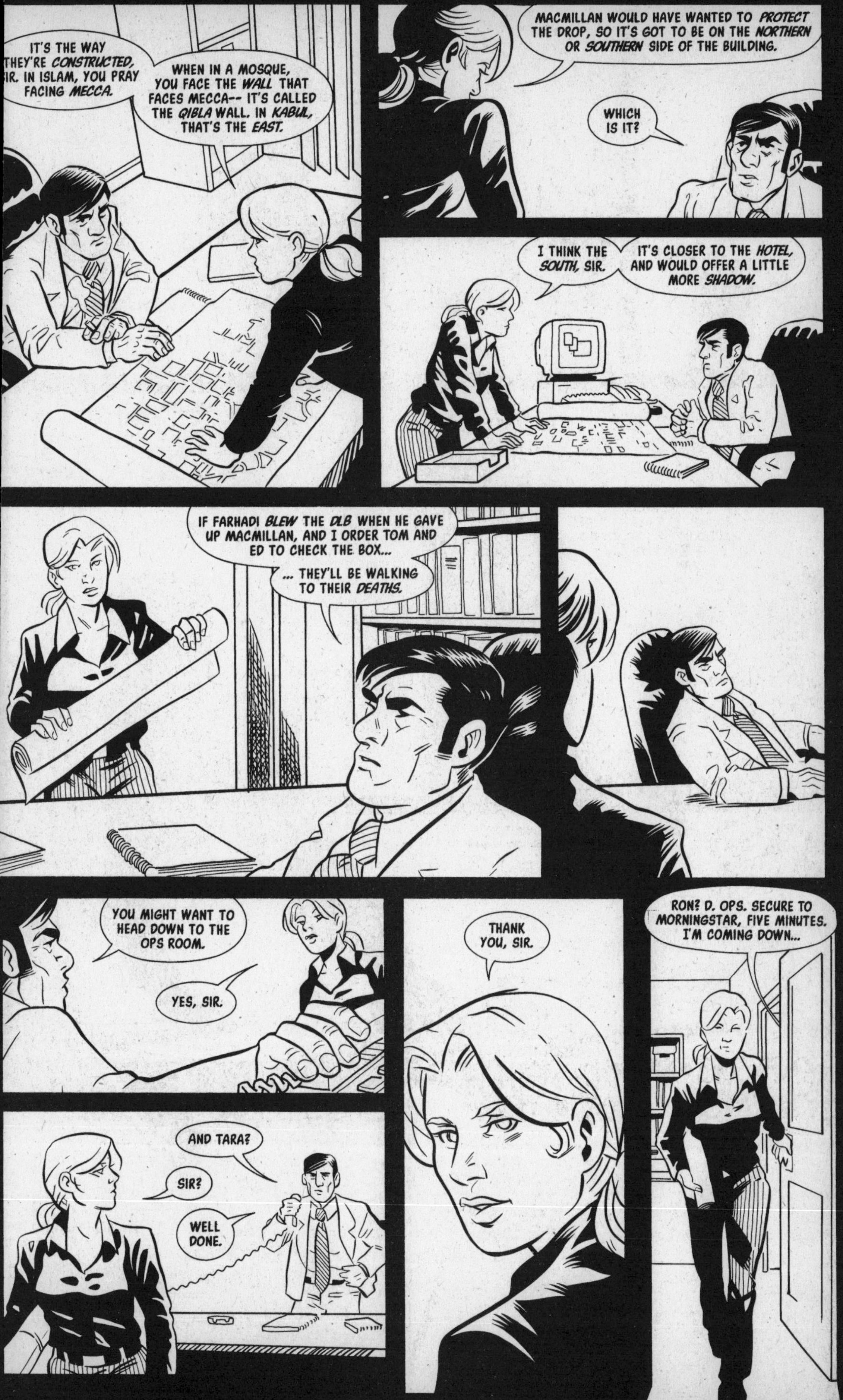
IT'S THE WAY THEY'RE CONSTRUCTED, SIR. IN ISLAM, YOU PRAY FACING MECCA.
WHEN IN A MOSQUE, YOU FACE THE WALL THAT FACES MECCA-- IT'S CALLED THE QIBLA WALL. IN KABUL, THAT'S THE EAST.
MACMILLAN WOULD HAVE WANTED TO PROTECT THE DROP, SO IT'S GOT TO BE ON THE NORTHERN OR SOUTHERN SIDE OF THE BUILDING.
WHICH IS IT?
I THINK THE SOUTH, SIR.
IT'S CLOSER TO THE HOTEL, AND WOULD OFFER A LITTLE MORE SHADOW.
IF FARHADI BLEW THE DLB WHEN HE GAVE UP MACMILLAN, AND I ORDER TOM AND ED TO CHECK THE BOX...
... THEY'LL BE WALKING TO THEIR DEATHS.
YOU MIGHT WANT TO HEAD DOWN TO THE OPS ROOM.
YES, SIR.
AND TARA?
SIR?
WELL DONE.
THANK YOU, SIR.
RON? D. OPS. SECURE TO MORNINGSTAR, FIVE MINUTES. I'M COMING DOWN...

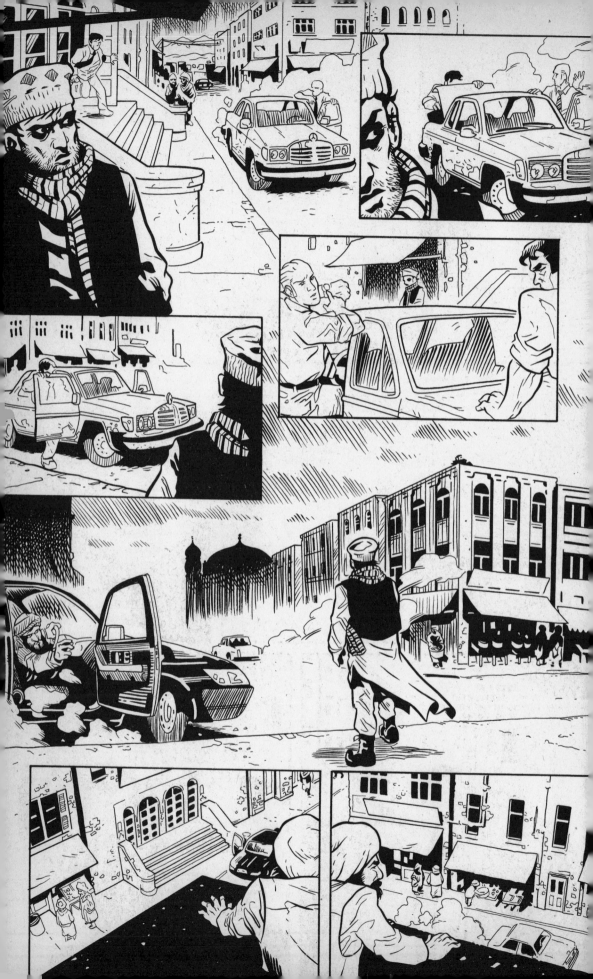

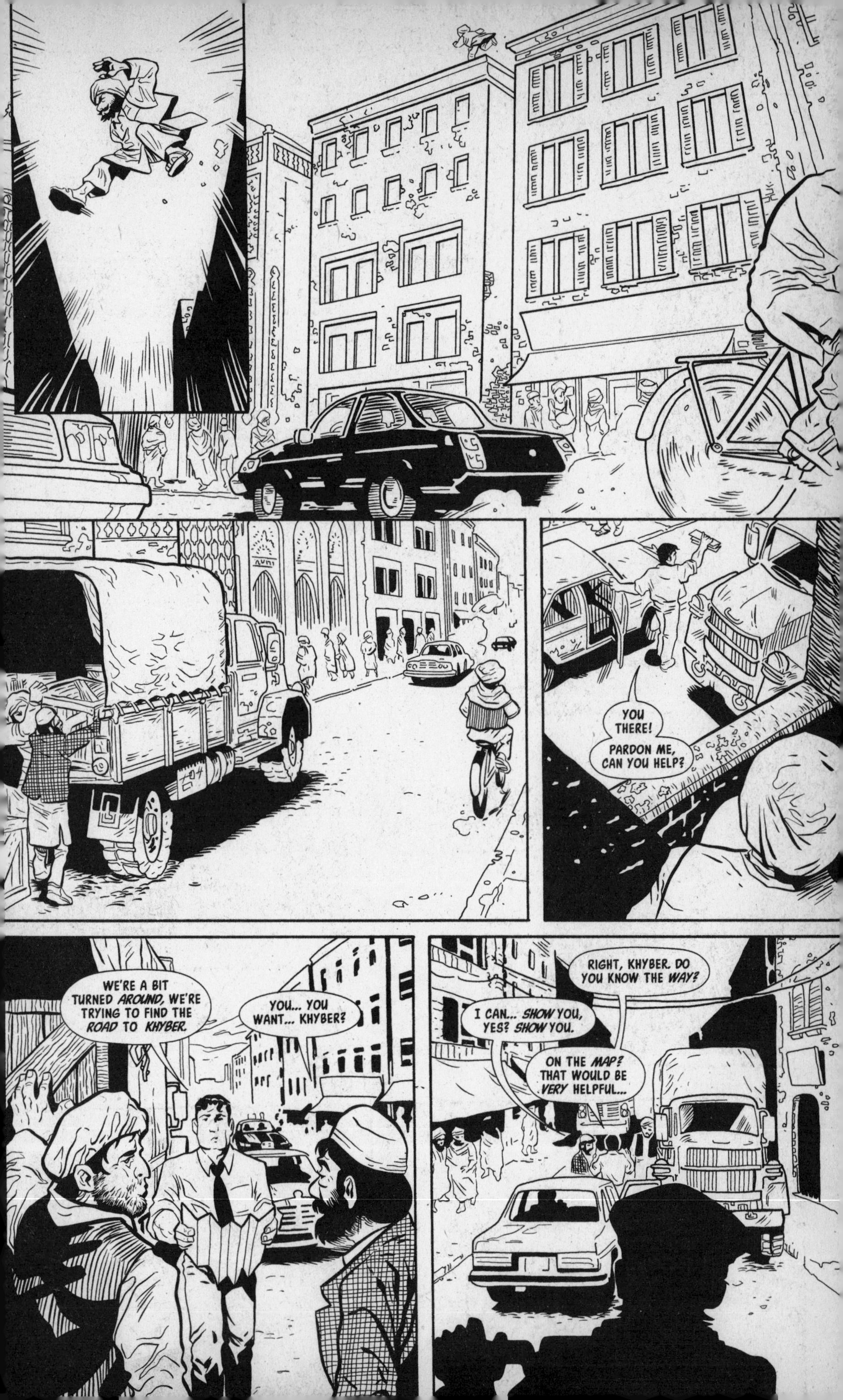
YOU THERE!
PARDON ME, CAN YOU HELP?
WE'RE A BIT TURNED *AROUND*, WE'RE TRYING TO FIND THE *ROAD* TO *KHYBER*.
YOU... YOU WANT... KHYBER?
RIGHT, KHYBER. DO YOU KNOW THE *WAY*?
I CAN... *SHOW* YOU, YES? *SHOW* YOU.
ON THE *MAP*? THAT WOULD BE *VERY* HELPFUL...

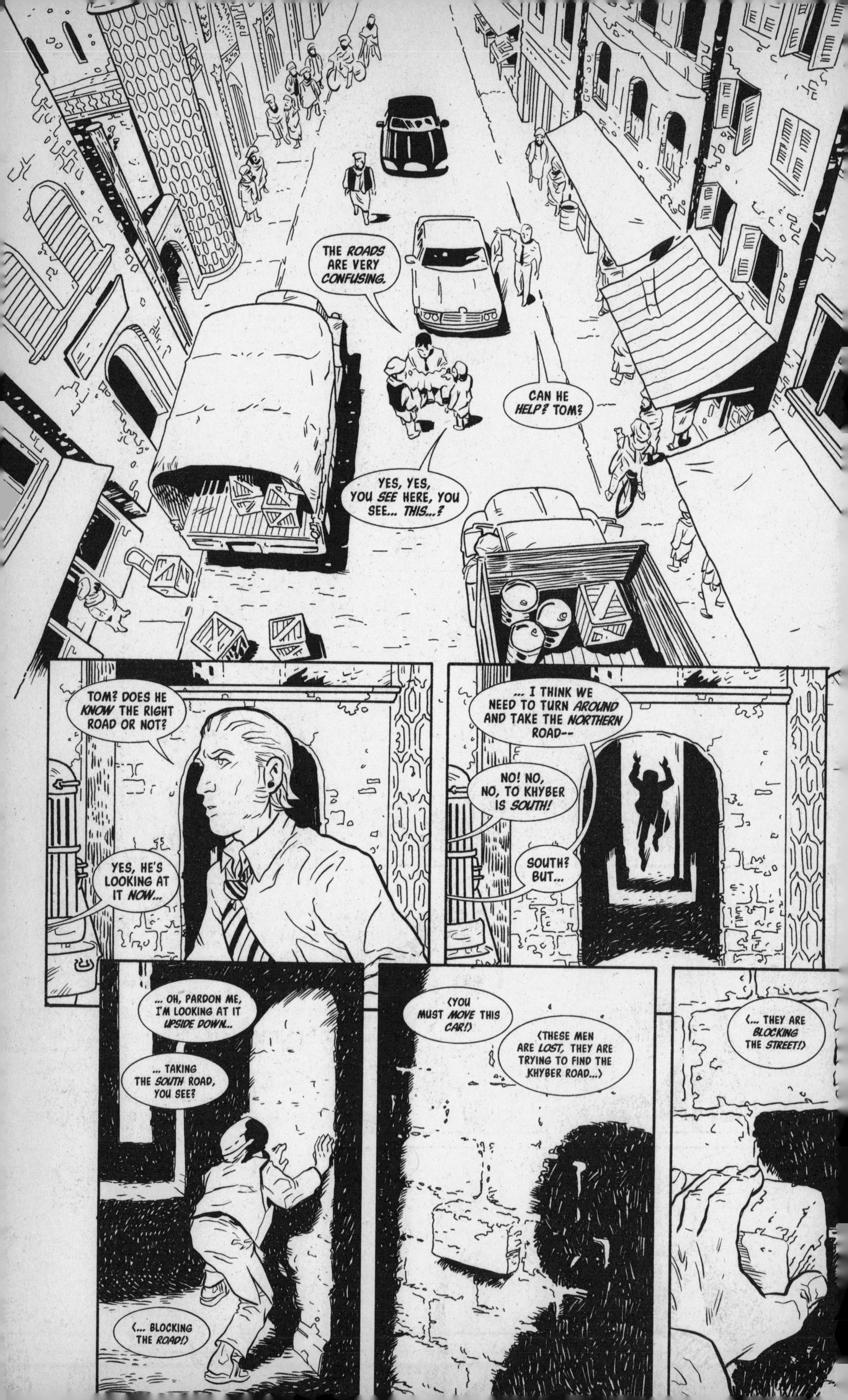
THE ROADS ARE VERY CONFUSING.
CAN HE HELP? TOM?
YES, YES, YOU SEE HERE, YOU SEE... THIS...?
TOM? DOES HE KNOW THE RIGHT ROAD OR NOT?
YES, HE'S LOOKING AT IT NOW...
... I THINK WE NEED TO TURN AROUND AND TAKE THE NORTHERN ROAD--
NO! NO, NO, TO KHYBER IS SOUTH!
SOUTH? BUT...
... OH, PARDON ME, I'M LOOKING AT IT UPSIDE DOWN...
... TAKING THE SOUTH ROAD, YOU SEE?
<... BLOCKING THE ROAD!>
<YOU MUST MOVE THIS CAR!>
<THESE MEN ARE LOST, THEY ARE TRYING TO FIND THE KHYBER ROAD...>
<... THEY ARE BLOCKING THE STREET!>

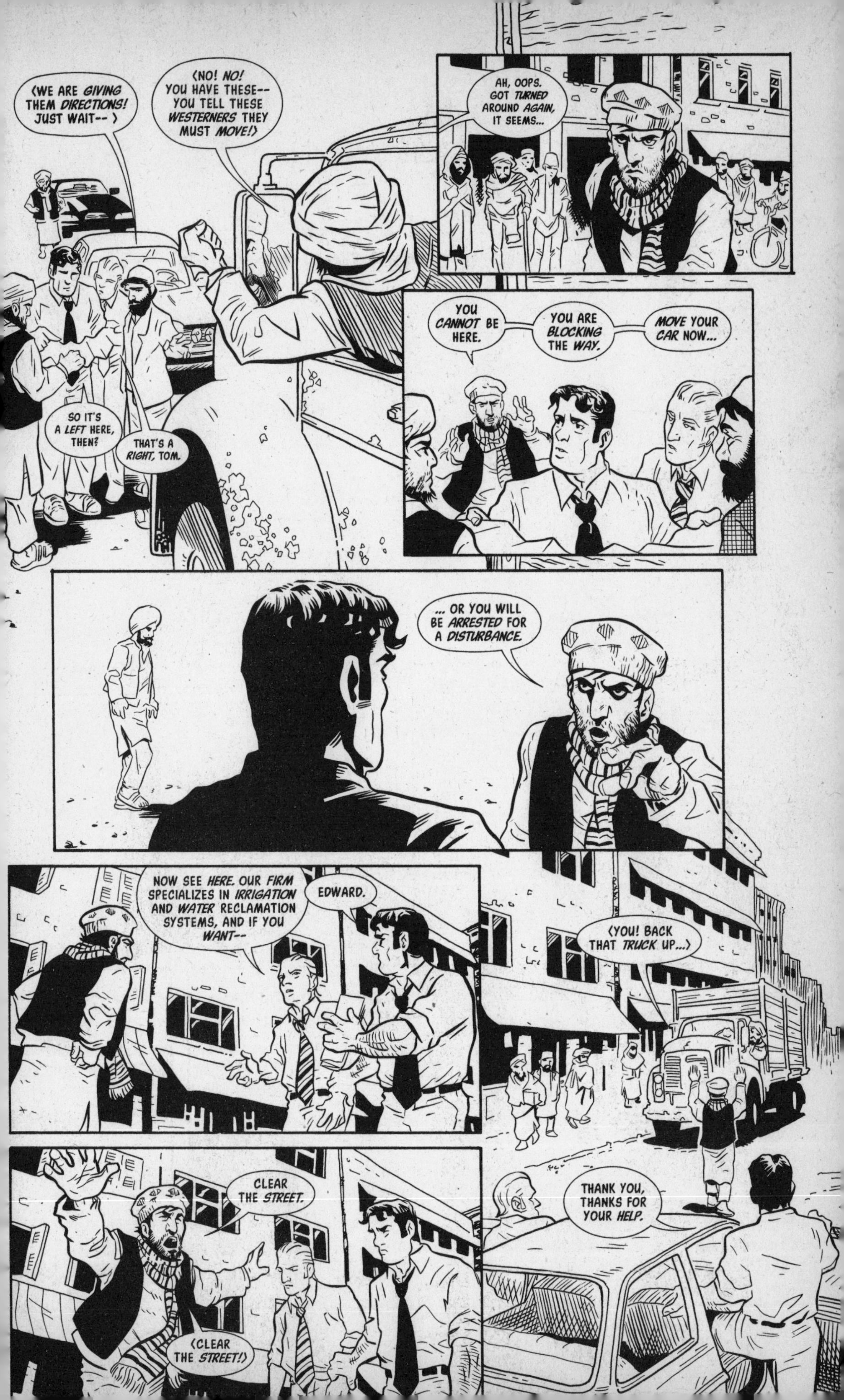

⟨WE ARE *GIVING* THEM *DIRECTIONS!* JUST WAIT-- ⟩
⟨NO! *NO!* YOU HAVE THESE-- YOU TELL THESE *WESTERNERS* THEY MUST *MOVE!*⟩
SO IT'S A *LEFT* HERE, THEN?
THAT'S A *RIGHT*, TOM.
AH, OOPS. GOT *TURNED* AROUND *AGAIN*, IT SEEMS...
YOU *CANNOT* BE HERE.
YOU ARE *BLOCKING* THE *WAY.*
MOVE YOUR *CAR* NOW...
... OR YOU WILL BE *ARRESTED* FOR A *DISTURBANCE.*
NOW SEE *HERE.* OUR *FIRM* SPECIALIZES IN *IRRIGATION* AND *WATER* RECLAMATION SYSTEMS, AND IF YOU *WANT*--
EDWARD.
⟨YOU! BACK THAT *TRUCK* UP...⟩
CLEAR THE *STREET.*
⟨CLEAR THE *STREET!*⟩
THANK YOU, THANKS FOR YOUR *HELP.*

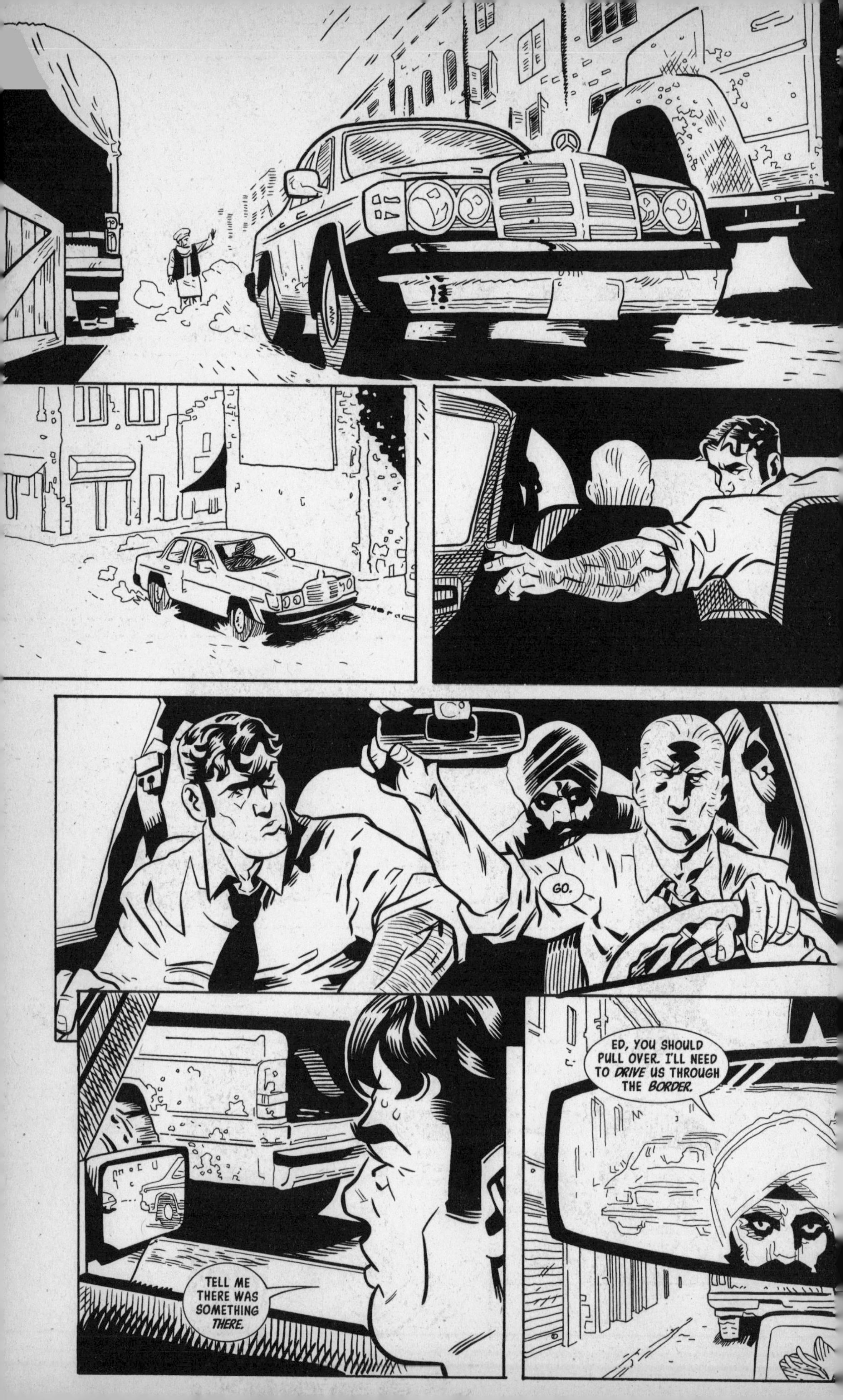
GO.
TELL ME THERE WAS SOMETHING *THERE.*
ED, YOU SHOULD PULL OVER. I'LL NEED TO *DRIVE* US THROUGH THE *BORDER.*

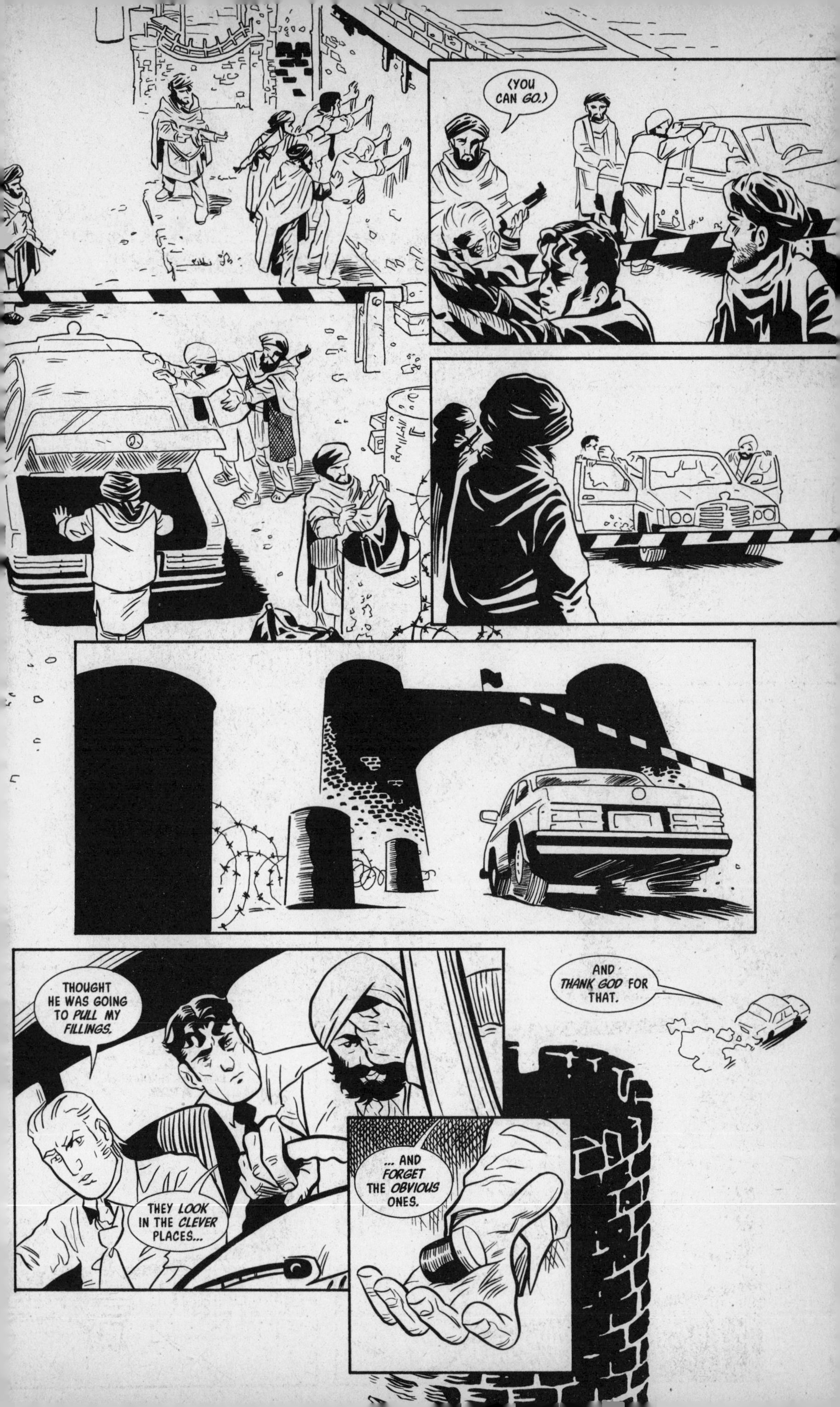

‹YOU CAN GO.›
THOUGHT HE WAS GOING TO PULL MY FILLINGS.
THEY LOOK IN THE CLEVER PLACES...
... AND FORGET THE OBVIOUS ONES.
AND THANK GOD FOR THAT.

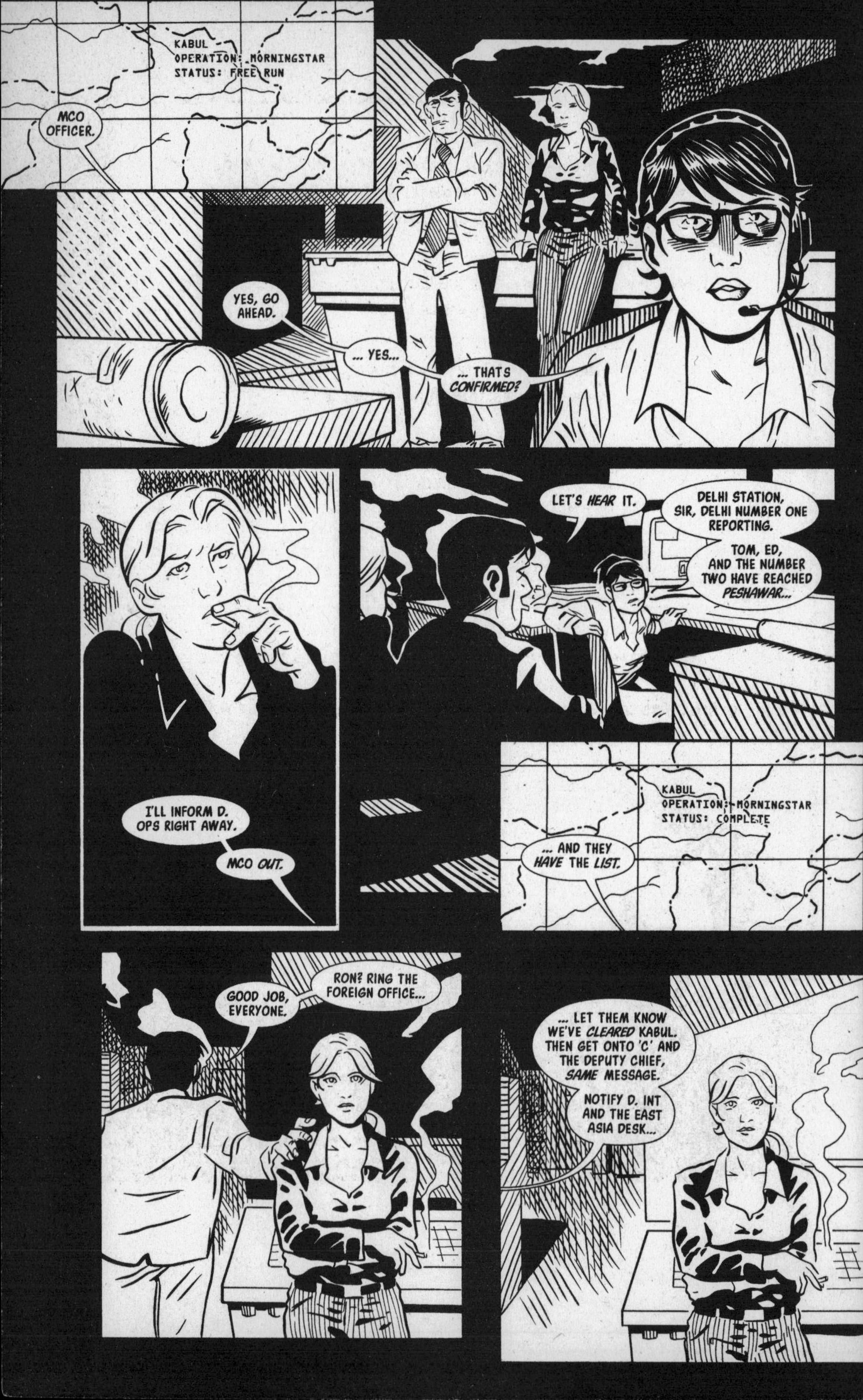
KABUL
OPERATION: MORNINGSTAR
STATUS: FREE RUN
MCO OFFICER.
YES, GO AHEAD.
... YES...
... THATS CONFIRMED?
LET'S HEAR IT.
DELHI STATION, SIR, DELHI NUMBER ONE REPORTING.
TOM, ED, AND THE NUMBER TWO HAVE REACHED PESHAWAR...
I'LL INFORM D. OPS RIGHT AWAY.
MCO OUT.
KABUL
OPERATION: MORNINGSTAR
STATUS: COMPLETE
... AND THEY HAVE THE LIST.
GOOD JOB, EVERYONE.
RON? RING THE FOREIGN OFFICE...
... LET THEM KNOW WE'VE CLEARED KABUL. THEN GET ONTO 'C' AND THE DEPUTY CHIEF, SAME MESSAGE.
NOTIFY D. INT AND THE EAST ASIA DESK...

For more information about issues discussed in this book, here is a brief list of some of the websites we used for research. Check them out, and stay informed.

The Revolutionary Association of the Women of Afghanistan (RAWA):
www.rawa.org

The Feminist Majority Foundation:
www.feminist.org/afghan/intro.asp

From Afghanistan Online—a U.S. based, non-governmental website—
a list of links about Women in Afghanistan:
www.afghan-web.com/woman/

The Committee to Protect Journalists:
www.cpj.org/index.html

U.S. State Department Report on Opium Production in
Afghanistan, as of December 2001:
usinfo.state.gov/regional/nea/sasia/afghan/fact/11dec00.htm

GREG RUCKA

Born in San Francisco, Greg Rucka was raised on the Monterey Peninsula. He is the author of several novels, including four about bodyguard Atticus Kodiak, and of numerous comic books. He has won two Eisner Awards for his work in the field, including one for *Whiteout: Melt* (Best Limited Series, 2000) and one for *Queen & Country* (Best New Series, 2002). Greg resides in Portland, Oregon, with his wife, Jennifer, and their son, Elliot. His next novel, *Fistful of Rain*, is due in 2003.

BRIAN HURTT

Brian Hurtt was born in Wichita, KS, and since then has traveled the world, only recently settling in St. Louis, MO. He began his career in comics in 2001, debuting as the second penciller of *Queen & Country*. He has since worked with Jen Van Meter and Jim Mahfood on a story for *Captain America* #50 and has been winning critical praise for his artistic collaboration with Arthur Dela Cruz on the Oni Press miniseries *Skinwalker*. Hurtt is currently hard at work on the *Queen & Country: Declassified* miniseries, set for a November release, and then for comics parts unknown (with Oni in tow).

BRYAN O'MALLEY

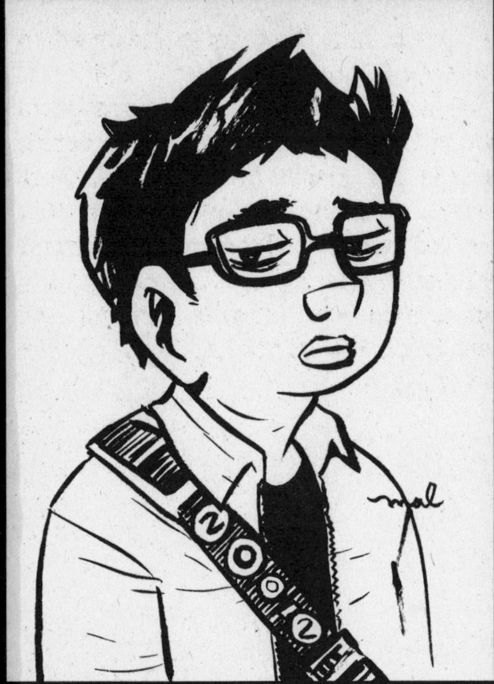

mal

Bryan O'Malley is from Canada and knows almost nothing about spies. He's only seen like one James Bond movie (*Live and Let Die*... oh wait, he also saw most of *From Russia With Love* one time), and he's never seen a single episode of *The Prisoner* even though his roommate keeps claiming that he has the entire series on VHS. Despite that, somehow he got this job, and then they let him letter *Blue Monday*, *Jason and the Argobots* and a variety of other things. He also has drawn *Hopeless Savages: Ground Zero* for Oni, written by Jennifer Van Meter, who is, incidentally, married to Greg. Of course, Bryan's own *Lost at Sea* appeared in the Oni *Color Special 2002* and will be a miniseries from Oni in 2003. And as if that wasn't enough, one can always find more from Bryan on the internet, at www.radiomaru.com.

CHRISTINE NORRIE

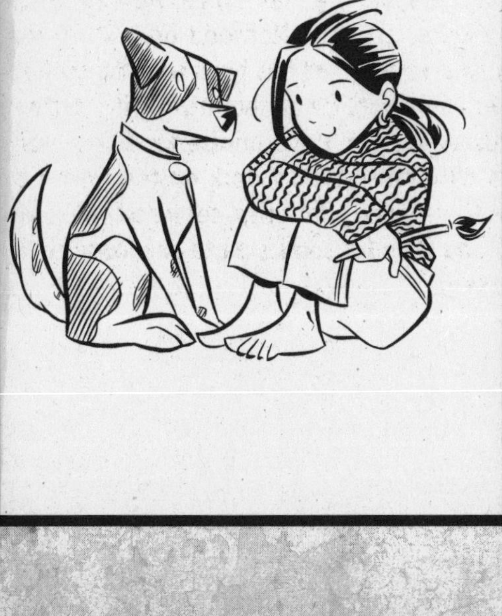

Christine Norrie's one true editor, Jamie S. Rich, has dubbed her "the most adorable thing in comics, and that's including Sugar and Spike." In addition to that, the resident of Staten Island, NY, is also an accomplished cartoonist, having created *Kung-fu Spacegirls* and the upcoming Oni Press projects *Cheat* and *Crush*. In 2001, she teamed with writer Jen Van Meter and tackled the main art chores on *Hopeless Savages*, helping to earn the book a 2002 Eisner Award Nomination for Best Limited Series and garnering herself a 2002 nomination for the Russ Manning Award. Her other main gig in this period was drawing the *Spy Kids* comic strips for *Disney Adventures Magazine*. Her website is spookoo.com, and features all sorts of sketches, ideas, and original thingamjigs. She lives with a dog named Orwell and a husband named Andy. In that order.

Other books from Greg Rucka and Oni Press

"*Greg Rucka is not a lesser writer. As an author, he thrives in political, moral and emotional complexity.*"

— Warren Ellis, creator of Transmetropolitan and Global Frequency

Queen & Country™ Vol. 1
Operation: Broken Ground
by Greg Rucka, Steve Rolston & Stan Sakai
128 pages • black-and-white interiors
$11.95 US • ISBN 1-929998-21-X

Queen & Country™ Vol. 2
Operation: Morningstar
by Greg Rucka, Brian Hurtt,
Bryan O'Malley, and Christine Norrie
88 pages • black-and-white interiors
$8.95 US • ISBN 1-929998-35-X

"*Whiteout's well researched, well written and expertly rendered. Don't buy it for those reasons, though. Buy it because Carrie Stetko's mouthy, freckled and cool…*"

— Kelly Sue DeConnick, artbomb.net

For a comics store near you, call 1-888-COMIC-BOOK or visit www.the-master-list.com.

For more information on more Oni Press books go to: www.onipress.com

Queen & Country™ Vol. 3
Operation: Crystal Ball
by Greg Rucka & Leandro Fernandez
144 pages • black-and-white interiors
$14.95 US • ISBN 1-929998-49-X

Queen & Country™ Vol. 4
Operation: Blackwall
by Greg Rucka & J. Alexander
88 pages • black-and-white interiors
$9.95 US • ISBN 1-929998-68-6

Queen & Country™ Vol. 5
Operation: Storm Front
by Greg Rucka &
Carla Speed McNeil
152 pages • black-and-white interiors
$14.95 US • ISBN 1-929998-84-8

Queen & Country™ Vol. 6
Operation: Dandelion
by Greg Rucka & Mike Hawthorne
120 pages • black-and-white interiors
$11.95 US • 1-929998-99-0

Whiteout™
by Greg Rucka & Steve Lieber
128 pages • black-and-white interiors
$11.95 US • ISBN 0-9667127-1-4

Whiteout: Melt™
by Greg Rucka & Steve Lieber
128 pages • black-and-white interiors
$11.95 US • ISBN 1-929998-03-1

Queen & Country™
Declassified Vol. 1
by Greg Rucka & Brian Hurtt
96 pages • black-and-white interiors
$8.95 US • ISBN 1-929998-58-9